Praise for *Safe*

"This is a very powerful book, and one that begs a deep understanding of the recovery process. It's all I can do to put it down and take a break. Thank you for putting this in print."

—Mark Baus, DVM, contributor to *Veterinary Clinics of North America: Equine Practice*

"With great courage and skill, Elspeth Roake has written a searing account of her battle with mental illness brought on by trauma. This subject matter has been much in the news, but those of us in journalism who try to cover it cannot hope to match the power of Ms. Roake's intimate account."

—Paul Friedman, television news executive

"A powerful story that not only tells the truth about mental illness, but also about how our passions help keep us grounded."

—Piper Klemm, Ph.D., publisher, *The Plaid Horse*

"A completely unrestrained, intimate, and triumphant account of one brave woman's battle with depression. *Safe* leaves you breathless in empathy with the often-invisible pain of mental illness. Ms. Roake invites the reader to join her on her complex journey of discovery and healing which is inherently interwoven with the rewards and challenges of working as a rider and groom on the hunter/jumper show circuit."

—Karen V. Robertson, co-writer of George Morris's *Unrelenting*

Safe

Elspeth Roake

Safe

a memoir

Brandylane
Publishers, Inc.
Publishing books since 1985

ISBN: 978-1-947860-86-5
LCCN: 2020911834

Designed by Michael Hardison
Production managed by Haley Simpkiss

Author photo (p. 247) by ESI Photography

Printed in the United States of America

Published by
Brandylane Publishers, Inc.
5 S. 1st Street
Richmond, Virginia 23219

 Brandylane
Publishers, Inc.
Publishing books since 1985

brandylanepublishers.com

To all my animals—past, present, and future.

1. The Hospital

I'm not Safe.

It starts as a hairline crack in my mind, and widens into a canyon I can no longer bridge. I know there must be a way to reunite the meaning of the word with the sensation—a feeling I seek recklessly as an addict chasing but never quite achieving their first high. I see shadows, but long for reality. I hang untethered over the expanse, reaching for a vantage point from which I might understand how a nonentity can ache so badly. All I want is to be safe. This is what it has amounted to.

I'm not sure how I ended up here. I know I followed my GPS to the nearest emergency room. I know I have been sitting and shaking in the parking lot for an hour. I know I've made several phone calls already: one to my on-again off-again psychiatrist, who is on the ski slopes of Utah, as far away from being able to help me in miles as in spirit; one to my best friend, who encouraged me to go inside; one to my parents, who encouraged me not to. And I know that I am now obsessively hitting redial, in an attempt to reach the only person in the world who has the power to help me, the power to make a difference: Leslie. She is my boss, the rock that keeps me grounded.

After the tenth call, she picks up and says she can't talk; she has dinner guests. I beg and plead, telling her that this time I mean it; I really, really am going to kill myself. She tells me we'll talk in the morning. I'm the girl who cries wolf.

I text my coworker and tell her I am probably not going to be able to come to work tomorrow, on account of the fact that Leslie, my protector, doesn't care that I'm suicidal. She responds with a heart and a message saying not to worry; she'll be fine taking care of the horses while I take care of myself.

I call my manager at her home a thousand miles away in Connecticut, and through incoherent tears demand to know why Leslie, who I am pretty sure would do anything for me, has abandoned me in my time of greatest need. Which, granted, is pretty much all the time.

"I don't have an answer for you, El," Jen says reasonably. "I know she does care about you, and has been worrying about you for some time. Perhaps she simply doesn't know how to help you anymore. Perhaps she wants to show you that at some point, the only person who can help you is you."

"That's a stupid risk," I wail. "How can she know what I'm feeling or what I'm capable of?"

"We both know you can do this. But right now, you need to walk into the ER, for no one but yourself. Call me later."

I thank her and continue to shiver in the front seat of the rental car, curled up tightly in an effort to contain the intolerable pain inside of me. Everyone is wrong. I have no ability to help myself. I need Leslie.

Eventually I get out of the car. Even at this late hour, heat radiates off the Florida pavement, and I welcome the discomfort in my layered sweaters. In the heat, I dress for air conditioning. My head hurts, and I keep staring at my phone, willing her to care.

As I approach the hospital's entrance, I am surprised by the number of locals milling about, and their general ethnic diversity. I've been to the ER in Connecticut, but this is downtown Ocala, Florida. These people are not northerners here for the winter horse-show circuit, as we are. It's easy to tell us apart from the year-round residents.

A sign above triage indicates the wait time is between twenty minutes and three hours, depending on the nature of the emergency. Based on my experience, I figure my wait time will be approximately three days, considering I'm not even sick. Huge red block letters spell out "Emergency" over the dirty, unwelcoming concrete facade. Is it an Emergency?

Without checking in, I go directly to the bathroom and cry over the fact that I don't want to live and don't have the courage to die. I call my parents again and tell them that against their advice, I am going to admit myself. I have run out of options. They are upset; they feel I am making the wrong decision. They're British; they think I can tough it out. But ultimately, they are still my parents, and they say they will support me no matter what. The insurance deductible will be around four grand, and as I am still paying off last year's, it goes unspoken that I will need their help. One more way in which I have failed.

Back in the waiting room, I assume the stance of a distraught but healthy family member and scan the crowd in an effort to assess my status among those waiting. All my life, my problems have been brushed off as insignificant or attention-seeking. Looking around the crowded emergency room, it's hard not to wonder if it's true.

I sit and try to tell myself that it's not that bad, that the weight of the past year isn't crashing down around me; but it doesn't work. I am ready to begin.

I walk up to the desk and tell the austere old lady behind it that I am suicidal, and that I want to be admitted for the night. Evenings and nights have always been the hardest hours for me. I know that if I can make it until morning, I have a fighting chance of getting through the next day.

The woman's condescending stare rests on me for uncomfortable seconds. A thick cloud of judgment hangs over her, though in fairness, I figure that's part of her job.

"Do you have a plan?" she asks morosely. Her glasses perch on the very edge of her nose, and her hair is piled into a beehive.

"Um, yeah, I guess?" What kind of question is that? Of course I have a plan. I've come here, haven't I? My plan is to get through the night without hurting myself, and I'm taking the necessary steps.

"Yes, or no?"

What does she want to hear?

"Yes?"

"Name?"

I must have passed. Fear and shame compete with the terror of being alive. *I'm trying, I think. I don't want to, but I'm trying anyway. There isn't a good choice. Please don't make it worse.*

She picks up a phone and informs a Henry that he is needed. As I deliberate over whether I should remain seated or relocate, Henry materializes. I put him around a hundred years of age, with a strong resemblance to Jesus Christ, had Jesus Christ lived that long.

"Follow me, dear!" he booms pleasantly. "Where are you from?"

"Um—Connecticut," I whisper. A friendly monologue about his aunt from Connecticut ensues. None of this feels real.

Inside the examination room, I curl up under the fluorescent lights and try to settle into the current of voices and activities around me. The bare and unforgiving plastic of the examination table presses up hard against me. *This is what I asked for*, I remind myself. *Someone or something, a place to protect me from myself.*

I am not thrilled to find my phone, book, and prescription medication put in a cabinet that is zip-tied shut, not with one zip tie, but with five. Cutting communication is a step further away from Leslie, the one person who has the ability to control the pain.

A nurse comes in to collect basic information, a different nurse to take vitals and draw blood. They are tired and busy, jaded by the job. *It's okay*, I tell myself. *Get through it, and soon you'll be left alone to focus on surviving the night.*

"Have you ever been Baker-Acted?" another angry-sounding nurse asks.

I have no idea what that means, but I don't have the strength to ask, so I just say no.

"You'll be on a minimum of an involuntary seventy-two-hour hold." Why is everyone so angry?

"No, I came in voluntarily." This isn't open for interpretation.

"Doesn't matter. You told triage you had a plan to kill yourself."

I did? I'm suicidal and self-destructive, but that's a long way from having a plan to die. If I truly had one, I'd get on with it instead of showing up for help. I just want supervision and safety until daybreak. Surely they'd like to free up my room for someone who is actually sick or hurt?

"I'd only like to stay the night." I can miss a little work Monday morning; that's the lightest day of the week. That way, even if it takes the better part of the morning to dig up a psychiatrist to sign me out, I won't have missed anything important. There is no such thing as calling in sick in the horse world. "That's what I do in Connecticut sometimes."

"Well, this is Florida. We do things differently down here. You'll stay in the ER until a bed opens up in a psychiatric hospital, which could be tomorrow or any time in the next week. It could be anywhere in the state of Florida, depending on availability. You'll stay there for a minimum of seventy-two hours, and after that, a doctor can release you as they see fit."

There's no way this is possible. "What if I leave against medical advice?" They can't force me to stay against my will.

"Won't work. If you walk out that door the police will be dispatched and you'll be arrested and detained until the matter can be taken up in court. No way out of this now."

Panic rises so fast and high that I fear I may drown in the deluge. Shock keeps me immobile and silent. *Arrested?* My worst fears have come true. Being depressed and suicidal really does make me a bad person. Asking for help was a mistake. I've used up the patience of all my friends, I'm too weak to fight for myself, and this is what I'm left with. I'm a bed in a system devoid of human elements. Between four days and forever. I've lost my sense of time—sense of trust—sense of self.

As scared as I am to be abandoned to my own devices out in the world, I've also developed a host of coping strategies to stay alive out there. I decompress in the presence of my horses; I work long hours; and on a good day, I can read and write and exercise. On a bad day, I open my skin with razor blades—not to die, but to lessen the pain. Without any of these resources, I have no chance. Then it hits me: I can't, absolutely and categorically, live without Leslie. I need her. *Now.*

"I need a phone." My voice belongs to someone I don't care to know.

"That's not really going to be possible."

"*I need a phone.*" I sound like an addict. I don't care. Nothing matters but this. I'd sell my soul.

Even the nurse can read my raw and naked terror. She sighs. "I'll see what I can do."

I lie there as if I have been dropped from a great height and landed in a mangled heap. Too paralyzed to generate the effort it would take to cry, I let the flood of tears slide down my temples on their own. They fill my ears, then overflow onto the hairline of my neck and pool around my shoulders. Maybe I will drown.

In my periphery, I see her rush back and forth, occupied by activities other than finding me a phone. But I have no words; my only language is the flow of tears.

After a while, the nurse rushes back into the room to write something down. She glances at me and asks if I'm okay. I couldn't be further from it. I summon everything I have to remind her about the phone.

She sighs again. "I can't find one to bring to you. I'll give you my hospital phone. Hit nine for the outside line. I'll be back in a few."

My hand is shaking so hard that it takes me four tries to get the right number—the only number I have memorized for emergencies. Leslie rarely picks up for an unknown number, and more often than not, she turns her phone off overnight. But when I hear her say hello, relief rushes life back into me.

"Help me; please help me, please, please!" Leslie can fix anything. She always has.

"Where are you?"

I've forgotten. In my hysteria, I'm slipping out of touch with reality. "I don't know! Please help me; I really, really need you!"

"No problem." The calm in her voice is my antidote. "Tell me where you are."

"At the hospital! Please, please! I'm . . . I'm locked up. I can't get out. I need help!"

"Okay. What's the name of the hospital?"

"I don't know!"

"Is there someone you can ask?"

"I don't know!"

"Is it written down anywhere in the room?"

I look around frantically. There is a framed poster on the wall. I think it might say something. I try to speak, but I'm crying so hard it's impossible. She's used to this.

"Maybe I could talk to someone. I'm sure there's someone around?"

As if on cue, the nurse returns for her phone.

"Please . . . tell her," I manage. To her credit, she takes the phone, and I hear a rational sequence of words, even if they have no meaning to me.

I collapse back onto my plastic coffin. Leslie will not come. She does not care if I die.

•••••

Time passes.

"Hi, baby."

My eyes fly open as I twist around to look. For a split second, the pain recedes.

"You came!" I start crying again, though I can't say whether I ever stopped. All tears are different.

"'Course I came."

"You came."

"Yup."

Seeing Leslie almost makes everything bearable. If she cares enough to come here in the middle of the night, maybe the world is a place I can live in.

"What's going to happen to me?"

"Well, you're going to stay here for a little bit, maybe wait until there's a space for you at a different hospital."

"Where?"

"I'm not sure yet. But it will be fine."

"But if it's far, you can't visit because you'll be at the horse show."

"True, but let's hope that it's not far."

"And if it is?"

"You'll find a phone."

"Are you mad?"

"I'm not mad. Have I ever been mad?"

"What about my job?" My job is my lifeline, the framework that gets me through each day. I get up because the horses need me.

"Well, you won't be able to work for a few days, but after that you'll be back. Same as usual."

"Am I fired?"

"Of course not."

"I'm scared."

"You know, El, sometimes things work out for the best. Maybe this isn't a bad thing. Maybe you needed to hit rock bottom to move back up the ladder."

"That's what I always think, and then it gets worse!"

"Worse than this?"

"I don't know."

"We're all here for you. You're going to make it."

"Okay."

"Do you want me to call your parents?"

I never ask for my parents.

"Yes, please."

"Do you want them to come?"

No.

"Yes."

Then she sits with me, softening the edges of the harsh and unfriendly room of plastic and pain. My despair cools from boiling to simmering. It's really all I ever want—someone to sit with me. Her. She does care, after all.

• • • • •

I sleep on and off for the next few days, finding a way to relax amid the rush of voices and piercing lights and thin acrylic sheets that are brought into the room for me. I can only measure time by guessing whether the meals I am served are breakfast, lunch, or dinner, and most of the time they are indistinguishable.

There is always someone sitting in a chair just inside my room. At first, I don't understand why, and it's irritating. One woman tries relentlessly to engage in small talk for far longer than is socially acceptable. I can't figure out who let this lonely old lady into the ER, or why chatting up a suicidal patient seems like a good idea to her. She seems to stay forever, but is finally replaced by a woman who spends hours screaming at the voice-to-text function on her phone. I wish I could tell her that raising the volume of her voice won't improve the program's accuracy.

Eventually it dawns on me: suicide watch. I am briefly pleased to be worthy of such procedures. But mainly, it makes me sad, because here is one more thing that should make me feel safe, but doesn't.

I ask for a tampon, and am told that the hospital doesn't provide these. I can't possibly be the first person to make this request. I ask my current keeper whether she can make an inquiry, but she says she isn't allowed to leave the chair. I ask the next nurse who comes in the same question, only to be dismissed again. Finally, I burst into tears, not so much because it matters to me if I lie in my own blood, but because this is what my life had been reduced to. I can't care for myself, but no one else can, either.

Nevertheless, I keep asking, out of stubbornness rather than desperation. Eventually, I am brought an adult diaper.

Why not, I think. I am locked up, isolated indefinitely in a fluorescent closet under the pretense of a guard. If I have to use the bathroom, I am escorted inside, my hospital-issue socks crunching and sticking to debris on the floor. All my life I have tried to convince myself that mental illness isn't a character flaw, that I shouldn't punish myself or be punished for being depressed. It turns out this isn't true after all.

Somewhere between waking and sleeping, I have the most

troubling thought of all: it has been quite some time since I've had either of my two antidepressant medications, both of which are zip-tied in the closet a few feet from the bed. It seems like a pretty grave oversight on the part of the staff, because at least three different people have asked me whether I am on any medication. I told all of them that I was, and that they took it from me, and that the first and last time I abruptly stopped an antidepressant, I became horribly sick.

I explain my dilemma to the next nurse who takes my vitals.

"Nothing we can do," she says. "We aren't authorized to dispense medication not prescribed here."

"So, can you prescribe it?"

"No. Only a psychiatrist can do that."

"I could give you the name of my psychiatrist. The contact information is in my phone."

"I can't give you your phone."

"So you expect me to stay here and get better, while withholding my medication? Would it be the same if I had a heart condition?"

"In that case, a doctor would make that determination. In your case, a request has to be processed through a psychiatrist. We have no authority to prescribe medication."

"But you don't have to prescribe it. It's two feet away, in a bottle from my pharmacy. You can watch me take one dose."

"We have no way of knowing what's really in the bottle."

"So, I can't have the medication I've been on for ten years. I'm in a hospital that withholds a treatment I have access to every day at home."

"No, one of our psychiatrists can write us a scrip for your current medication."

"So can he do that now?"

"No, he's not in today."

"And when will he be in?"

"Probably tomorrow."

"I can have my meds first thing tomorrow?"

"Probably not first thing. He has other appointments, but I'll put in a request for you to be seen if he has time."

"So there's really no way of knowing if or when I'll be able to have it."

"Like I said, I have no authority in that regard."

I can't get my head around the absurdity of it. I'm in no position to advocate for myself, and these people are actively trying to hurt me.

Sometime later, I find a young nurse standing over me, asking me if there is anything I need. I'm sure I don't make sense, but I try to tell her about the medication problem. I'm aware that I sound crazy. Is this the way it happens? If you're treated like you're crazy, do you become crazy trying to prove otherwise?

"Yeah, she's right. We can't prescribe them."

"But they're right *there*." I point halfheartedly to the cabinet.

"I see. This really isn't allowed, but I'm going to open that up and let you take today's. But I'm swamped right now, but I'll be back as soon as I can." She's pretty, in a frazzled way. Perhaps she is new and has not yet been overrun by the system.

I try to feel relieved and grateful, but I'm too overwhelmed. I'm afraid she'll forget, and her shift will end before I can get my medication.

Several hours later, I get up and walk over to the door, leaning my upper body into the hallway as far as the guard will tolerate. I wait. Eventually, I see the nurse rushing along the hallway.

"Shoot, I'm really sorry. We're so understaffed. I'll be right back with scissors to cut the zip ties."

When she returns, she tells me she needs to find the custodian: before she can open the cabinet, she needs to make sure she has new zip ties with which to close it. I try to see the humor in all this, but it isn't possible.

The nurse comes through with the zip ties, and reminds me again that this is against policy. I'm embarrassed to be so helpless, so completely at someone else's mercy. My clothes smell of horse, I haven't showered in days, my eyes are swollen halfway shut, and I'm wearing an adult diaper.

Still, I manage to thank her.

• • • • •

My parents come. I am both happy and mortified to see them. I have been hiding the severity of my condition for a long time. This is out of context for them. I don't want them to believe that I have failed. They gave me a perfect life, and I've managed to screw it up.

They are sympathetic and concerned, and my humiliation grows. They ask why I chose to come to the ER in the first place. I can't come up with anything, so for once I don't pretend.

"I wasn't safe."

"Why not? Safe from what?"

"I don't know."

"Can you be more specific? I'm not sure we understand."

"I just wasn't safe." I sound absurd, even to myself.

"But you are safe now, right?"

"Yes." I'm not. But it's what they need to hear, and I want to be able to give them something.

They question the staff and receive the same answers. If they bypass my insurance and pay out of pocket, I will be able to move to a psych facility down the road. One with a good reputation. They can afford it, but that doesn't lessen the guilt.

Having been told they will not be allowed to see me again—they had to bully their way past the front desk the first time—they hit the road back to North Carolina. It hurts to see them go, even though I felt uncomfortable with them here.

I go back to sleep; it's the only thing to do. When I wake, I try to gain hope from the fact that this might indeed be rock bottom. But I've thought this too many times before, and too many times I've been proven wrong.

My next guardian is a polite and quiet Hispanic woman who reads her book. I have gotten used to being watched peeing. I have quite a few hours before I need to start the quest for my next dose of medication. For now, I accept the futility of my situation, and settle back into the low-grade discomfort that I'm comfortable with.

I glance at the woman in the chair and try to feel a bit better on account of the presence of someone whose job it is to make sure I stay alive. I am no longer responsible. For years I've asked to be taken seriously. Now there is a live body acknowledging my desire to self-destruct, and who will in theory prevent me from doing so. But in the end, I only care about Leslie caring.

The Hispanic woman wakes me up. There's been a new development.

"You're being moved."

My heart jumps in surprise and a little fear. "Where?"

"The psychiatric facility in Ocala. It's not far. I think your dad got you in. I think this is very good."

I feel myself clench, trying to control the blender inside me. My insides are being chopped up and liquified by fear.

"You're a wonderful patient; I'm sure you'll be great over there. Good luck?" Why is that a question? I smile at her.

Two tough-looking men wearing blue uniforms stand in the hallway: my escorts. They are wide and tall and imposing. I manage to find a small amount of humor in the situation: I'm as weak as I have ever been, just over a hundred pounds and dizzy from lying down for so long. I'm wearing a hospital gown that doesn't close in the back (no drawstrings for me) and my diaper. One of my hands clutches the hospital-issued bag full of my belongings, and the other holds the gown closed behind my back.

I shuffle between the two men, one of my loose and dirty socks slipping to my toes. It's quiet, and we don't speak, as if this is a covert operation.

We leave out a back entrance. As I exit the building, the change in the air hits me. It's warm and humid, but wonderfully pleasant to be outside. February in Florida. I feel naked and exposed. It's still dark. I can feel the texture of the pavement under my feet, and the world is surreal. I ask what time it is.

4:35 a.m.

It hadn't occurred to me to wonder how we were going to get to the psychiatric hospital, so I am shocked to find I will be transported by ambulance. One of the men gets in the driver's seat, and the other climbs in the back with me.

It's my first time in an ambulance. I've spent so long trying to convince the world that I want to be treated as someone who has a physical illness. Now I'm in this ambulance, and it seems I have succeeded. I am worthy of the life-saving equipment all around me. I experience a strange moment of fear and euphoria. Have I won, or lost?

The guy in the back is friendly. He tries to make small talk, and I am so grateful he isn't telling me I don't belong here that I oblige him. He says he has a friend who works over at the horse show, and that he's always liked horses. Everyone says that. *A lot of work, though,* he ponders; *long hours.* Yes. I wish I was back at the show, even though I was miserable there—the eternal hope that a change in physical location will make a difference.

So, he asks, *how did you go from showing horses to ending up here?*

I smile and shrug. It's as good an answer as any.

It occurs to me that I never put myself in situations where I'm alone with a man. He could hurt me, rape me, and no one would know. No one would believe me; I'm the crazy one.

Then I realize I don't care at all. I'm not sure anything could hurt more than I already do. Maybe all I can hope for is variety in pain.

We arrive, and the man I've ridden with lets me in through a door labeled "Baker Act Entrance." Apparently there's a whole entrance for people who end up in my situation.

The man puts me in a waiting room, wishes me good luck in my recovery and in my job, and leaves. I like him for at least trying not to be a jerk.

The room is empty, clean, and bare—perhaps the most sterile room I have ever been in, nothing but off-white walls, off-white plastic chairs, and me, in my off-white hospital gown that doesn't close in the back. There's a glass window looking into an office, but it's abandoned.

I sit down and wait. I look forward to lying down in a real

bed, maybe eating a little breakfast, and talking to a friendly social worker.

There is no clock, but I know that I wait for a very, very long time. The chair is uncomfortable, and despite my exhaustion, I'm wide awake thanks to the ambulance ride and the hope of improved conditions. I listen for movement, and occasionally hear soft footsteps outside, but no one enters.

I try the two doors. Unsurprisingly, both are locked.

Anxiety starts seeping into the hopefulness. What if no one knows I'm here?

I work on trying to relax. Everything's going to be fine. I wouldn't have been brought here at five in the morning if a bed wasn't available; if there weren't staff on the premises. My head hurts badly. I close my eyes and try to allow time to pass. Panicking will make it worse. Still, with each passing minute, my chest tightens, and I am less able to remain calm.

When the door opens, my breath catches. It's my friend from the ambulance.

"What are you still doing here?" he asks, good-natured. I can only raise my eyebrows, as if it makes any difference.

Behind the man is a young woman about my age. She looks defiant and masculine and is wearing a bandage mid-arm. I sense phenomenal defeat emanating from her, and although we do not exchange words, I sympathize with her immediately.

Not long after the novelty of no longer being alone wears off, another woman enters, dragging a man with her. He doesn't smell drunk, but on the way in, he collapses onto the floor and lies motionless. The woman exclaims in a shrill voice, asking him whether he's alright.

Of course he's not, I want to say. But the man's escort manages to get him into a chair, where he moans and slumps sideway, and then makes her exit.

The fear returns full force. This man could be dying, and no one is concerned. What kind of place is this? I'm in a hospital, I'm terrified of the unknown and the uncertain, and with each passing second, I feel increasingly unwell. The three of us sit in silence, each locked in our own private hell.

Suddenly, lights come on inside the office, and sleepy-looking employees enter and start turning on computers. I peer through the window to catch a glimpse of the clock on their wall I am shocked to see that it's nine a.m.

I wait for something to happen. When nothing does, I get up the courage to bang on the glass.

A frowning woman slides the window open. In a bored tone, she informs me that the staff will get to us as soon as possible. We're not normal, after all. We're expected to act out, justified or not. She does, however, unlock the bathroom.

I go in and close the door, crouch down on my heels, and wrap my arms around my knees, trying to disappear inside myself. I sob so hard, I have to lean against the wall to keep my balance. In my entire life, I have never felt so alone, desperate, and hopeless. I want to stop feeling.

At last, I am led down a hallway to my final destination. I feel slightly less frantic, and the tears freefall in silence.

My newest escort unlocks a door with her fingerprint and motions me inside, but does not follow. As the door latches behind me, I look out onto a scene of chaos.

I stand frozen, trying to get past the high-pitched voice of someone singing a familiar tune with the words changed to expletives at full volume. The others in the common area seem either catatonic or manic. It looks like a large waiting room, with plastic chairs and coffee tables draped with ancient magazines. The inhabitants have lost their minds waiting.

I try to figure out what I'm supposed to do, where I'm supposed to go. I want a bed. The best-case scenario at this point is to lie down and wait it out.

I approach what looks like a nurses' station, where three frazzled women are trying to ward off a number of patients. There is no decorum, from either the staff or the inmates. I stand behind them, as if in line. When a nurse hurries out from behind the counter, I cut into her path and try to form words.

"I'd—I'd like a room. Please."

"You know you're only allowed in the rooms overnight. They're locked during the day. You have to stay in the common area," she retorts.

"I—I just got here. I don't know what I'm supposed to do."

This stops her for a split second.

"Well, in that case, you need to fill out forms at the nurses' station." She makes it sound as if this is my penance.

I turn back toward the mayhem and, seeing no way to bully my way into it, lean back against the wall and slide down it, dissolving into a puddle on the floor. I will stay here for the rest of my life. I could even see myself doing something completely irrational, like licking the walls, because now I really do feel insane.

I'm filling out forms, even though I'm not sure how I'm supposed to answer the questions they pose. Each question is scored from one through ten, one being "great" and ten being "awful." I create a consistent pattern of fours though sixes, fearing that if I let them know how I really feel, I'll never be let out. Still, at this point, I can't exactly fake being fine: I'm using the counter to hold myself upright, and can no longer be bothered to keep my gown held shut. I have been reduced to an adult toddler.

The nurse who grabs my forms motions for me to follow her through a door into a private cubicle.

What happens next shouldn't catch me off guard, but it does. I wish I was the type of person who could shut down or go numb under stress, yet for me it has always been an emotional escalation, and this is the crescendo. I am cavity searched.

• • • • •

I am allowed to shower, and given my clothes and books. I exchange my diaper for a sanitary pad. I will receive my medication once my forms have been processed, so all in all, I will have missed only a few doses. I will also have access to a phone for outgoing calls, provided I am granted permission to use it.

That is as far as the improvements go. Because I have just arrived and am not permitted to visit the cafeteria for twenty-four hours, my food is brought to me. I have a feeling it has been many hours since I last ate, so I make myself swallow the mystery meat atop bread that is so stale it feels toasted but I draw the line at the green strips of rubber posing as beans. I do sample the dyed sugar water. I am determined to maintain some level of strength.

Time isn't normal. I have already spent a few days in the ER, but my seventy-two-hour hold has not yet begun. How can I make it begin so that it can end? And when it ends, will it begin again?

After lunch is break time, followed by snack time, followed by smoking time, circling back around to break time. I don't smoke, and therefore am not allowed to go outside. Most of the day consists of the time between activities and the inactivity of the activities themselves. The sedentary nature of the day is detrimental to me. My coping strategies have always been of an active nature—anything to avoid sinking into the quicksand of depression.

There are groups, at least. I'm familiar with groups, when a moderator leads a discussion on a topic universal to most mental health patients. Participation is encouraged, and the idea is that the patients will learn from each other what does and does not work. For many, there is something comforting in sharing common battles, or hearing the horror of challenges not personally faced. We are given worksheets calling for written accounts of feelings, goals, or difficulties, with the expectation that good communication and analysis will lead to clarity and resolution. It's basically Life Skills 101 for those to whom living doesn't come naturally.

I've certainly failed in some critical way, but even good groups were never that helpful to me. Verbalizing, processing, and analyzing are already second nature to me. As for the human element, I just don't care.

These groups are an informal affair. Often the moderators are called to emergencies and we are left to our own devices. In one group, we listen to music. In another, we listen to a meditation recording. We also spend a lot of time coloring with broken crayons.

I don't consider myself judgmental, and I respect whatever strategies are necessary to survive or recover. I'm not opposed to trying something different, and I am open to new concepts, or even to reframing old ones. But I don't need to be in a hospital to try art therapy, listen to recordings, or list my strengths and weaknesses. I am highly motivated and independent—so much so that I am often unable to convince people I am depressed. I go to great lengths to pursue anything and everything that has even the slightest chance of helping me; yet I know the proverbial Band-Aid they are offering me is not going to close the severed artery of my soul.

I try to look forward to something called recreation period, but it is cancelled the first two days. Then, finally, the recreation counselor appears. She gives us each a yoga mat and asks us to sit down.

"Today we're going to go around the room, and each of you is going to tell me all the ways you stay active in your life." She has a sweet voice and a hyperactive smile that makes her seem a little dazed and confused.

She starts with me, and I know I set a high bar. "I run, swim, bike, weight lift, and, oh yeah, I have my job, where I ride and take care of horses twelve hours a day."

"That's wonderful!" she squeals. "Is there anything you'd like to add to that in the future?"

"Seems like enough."

"Great! Next?"

Twenty-five minutes later, recreation period ends, without us having moved at all. Either this is preschool, or I'm missing the point completely. Even in preschool, you get to run around.

Now that I'm more aware of my surroundings, it bothers me that the staff are all black and the patients all white. I could draw a multitude of conclusions there, but really, it's just one more thing that seems wrong.

The highlight of the day is a visit from a nutritionist who

serves food in the kitchen. His presentation consists of teaching us how to read nutrition labels—which he does by turning over food products and reading the words and numbers on the back aloud to us—and concludes with the distribution and consumption of the stale goods. He wears a hair net.

• • • • •

I understand that I need help, that it's not entirely a mistake that I ended up here. I've been depressed most of my life, and suicidal for most of the past year. Over the past few weeks, I have become an active danger to myself. But I am accustomed to a large degree of autonomy, and with that, I have managed to keep myself alive and functioning for thirty years.

I'm not sure what I am doing wrong. My problems are of a deep and complicated nature—but in the end, we are all miserable people who can't quite figure out how to function in the world. I try so hard to find meaning in the activities, to partake in the projects, and to give everything my full effort. I don't fit into society—but I don't fit in here either. My ultimate fear is that *this is it:* I am hospitalized, but even that isn't going to come close to helping me. There's nothing left.

I try to connect. In the outside world I feel as if I'm the only person imprisoned by my own pain, but here I am among fellow sufferers. They are not the lunatics I perceived them to be upon my arrival. They are smart and kind and sensitive, not at all opposed to sharing or listening without judgment. There's Erin, the alcoholic, who is young and beautiful and friendly, her gold hair tumbling around her smile. There's Sam, the lesbian from the waiting room, who has just lost her wife. There's Renee, who has been in a wheelchair for two years due to a fractured femur—the result of an accident she sustained in the military. Because of a botched surgery, she may never walk again, so she swallowed a bottle of Vicodin. There is Emily, who scratched three lines onto her arm, and Dustin, who recently took her only daughter off life support.

I acknowledge and respect their varying degrees of suffering, but still can't understand or place my own. When Renee asks me what my story is, I just shake my head. I can't bring myself to interact in a meaningful way. I feel even more alone.

During break time, smoking time, and the times when the activities or groups threaten to drive me nuts, I read a book. I dread coming to its end, so I reread each page three or four times. The days move at a snail's pace, and the pain inside me pulses steadily, like blood under a wound. The evenings are excruciating, the pain exploding upward in sudden spurts. Each time, my head spins in a nauseating rotation. My heart and lungs seem to stop working, and it takes me several minutes to regain my composure.

The phone becomes the focal point of my days. It is kept behind the nurses' station. At this point, I am so desperate to hear Leslie's voice that my hands shake violently, and I waste valuable time redialing the code and the number over and over again before I get it right. Our conversations are all the same— on my end, a frantic struggle to keep my emotions under control and avoid losing phone privileges; on her end, the same calm and rational responses as always.

"It's me." I barely manage to breathe out the words.

"Hi! How's it going?"

"I can't say."

"Because you don't know, or because you're being monitored?"

"The second."

"That bad?"

"Worse."

"Wow. Have you talked to anyone, like a counselor?"

"No."

"Are you going to?"

"Don't know."

"Are they feeding you?"

"A bit. Leslie. You don't understand."

"Worst experience ever?"

"You have no idea." I want to crawl inside the phone line.

"Okay. Hang in there and call me when you can."

"Bye."

I hang up my lifeline and miss her even more intensely than I did before. I don't know why I keep calling when every time I hang up it feels like I'm losing her all over again.

I begin to barter with myself. If I can get out, I promise I'll start taking my mental health seriously. I have no idea what that might entail, but I will make whatever commitment I need to. But first, I have to get out.

I call my parents and beg them to do something.

"But we went to great lengths to get you in. There's nothing we can do now you're in the system. If you want to get out, you have to get better."

I know that won't happen here.

Gradually, I come to accept that I only have one choice: deception. I've tried to come across as normal all my life, and now it's showtime. If I put my mind to it, I can outthink my captors. I came in weak and defeated, and have been made increasingly more so each day, but there are no other options.

I become flawlessly polite and cheerful. I participate in groups with astute and discerning reflections, causing everyone to nod in somber accord. When others speak, I make a display of putting down my book and hanging on their every word.

"You look much better than when you arrived," one patient comments. My new persona is not one to sob naked on the floor.

"Yes!" I exclaim. "I've learned so much from being here. I'm better now." I scan the room for the aides who wander around with clipboards, tracking the patients like they are a foreign species. I figure in this case, the aides' incompetence will work in my favor. I imagine them writing, *Ready to be released into the wild.*

However, as I come to learn from the other patients, the aides, nurses, janitors, supervisors, and cafeteria staff have nothing at all to do with the discharge process. The only ones who have any say in our fates are the psychiatrists.

I try the nurses' station. "I would like to see a psychiatrist when possible," I say with all the deference in the world.

It has no effect.

"Everyone meets with one in their first twenty-four hours here," the nurse recites blandly.

"Thank you. I understand," I say reasonably. "I think I've been here three or so days, and I haven't seen one." Three days? It feels like it's been three decades.

The nurse turns and looks at a clock on the wall. "He must be running late. He'll get to you."

Running three days late?

"You should have seen this one girl."

I turn to see a hefty woman hovering behind me. I think she's the patient who was singing when I arrived.

"She was sick—like really sick, like pneumonia or something. She had a really high fever. She'd been asking to see a doctor for almost a week, but it never happened. When she got discharged, she started screaming that the first thing she was gonna do when she got out of the hospital was go find a doctor. Ha! Funny, right? But not for her. She was real sweet, too. Always trying to make everyone else happy."

I stare at her with a sinking feeling that starts slowly, then suddenly intensifies. *This is bad,* I think. I could tear down the walls and set the place on fire, or I could be the model of equanimity and composure, but neither would make any difference at all. I am starting to think I might need a lawyer, but perhaps that is a privilege reserved for inmates in prison.

Finding a doctor becomes my new pastime. During our constant breaks, I watch the door. Whenever someone unknown enters, I find a way to inquire after their position. I ask patients and nurses, listen in on conversations, or simply approach the newcomers with, "Excuse me, Doctor?"

I have high hopes for one smartly dressed lady, but when I try, "Are you a doctor?" I receive a stare that could shatter glass and a sharp "Mind your own business!" in response. I think I have succeeded when I see a friendly-looking African American man in a white coat. When I approach him with my usual questions, he says, "I sure am a doctor—but not a psychiatrist." If only I had pneumonia.

It is recreation period, and we are once again seated on the yoga mats. This time, the activity involves glitter. Instead of partaking, I do push-ups—which I consider a more appropriate recreational activity—until I suddenly hear my name being called.

I look up to see a smiling Indian man standing by the door.

He has even pronounced my name correctly, which few people do.

I leap up, beaming. This is it. I know right away we're going to get along. I'm like that; I know right away.

The man leads me to a cold, empty room. It feels refreshing after doing push-ups in the stuffy common area. I can feel my blood flowing through me. This is my chance, and I'm not going to blow it.

The next twenty minutes are the best I've spent at the hospital. I get the impression I have been heard after answering only a handful of questions, though to this day I don't know how. Perhaps sometimes people are just compatible, although I rarely connect with men. I do put on a show, but I find I truly like and respect this man, which makes sincerity easier. I tell him about the miscommunication with the triage nurse in reference to my "having a plan." I admit to having had a bad night and feeling overwhelmed, but soften the severity of my experience. I concede to having been a cutter, but explain that it is no longer something I resort to regularly. He reads between the lines and chooses to let it go.

I rattle on about my coping strategies, which are well-developed and effective, if not always enough to slay the dragon. To the question of abuse and whether I am often suicidal, I say no. Despite my tentative trust, I know I'll never see him again.

When the doctor asks whether I can name some reasons for staying alive, I go on and on, and is real and true. He asks me about my goals, and I become genuinely lively, telling him about the triathlon I completed, the book I want to write, and the mentoring program in which I hope to participate. This is in addition to all my work and horse-showing goals.

The doctor seems thrilled, but I wonder if I have overdone it—not because what I've said hasn't been truthful, but because it's inconsistent with my being here. Not many can reconcile who I am on paper with a person who's hell-bent on self-destructing. But he seems to understand. When we part, he suggests something that stays with me.

"As you are pursuing all your goals and moving forward, stay cognizant of what they are masking, and why you feel the need to push yourself so hard. Ask yourself what you're running from; what you're trying to make up for." This idea has crossed my mind before, but I like who my goals make me into. I don't want to lose that part of me.

The doctor says he will sign the paperwork to start my discharge, but it will take a couple of days to go through. I decide to push my luck.

"Is there any way you could make it happen tomorrow morning? It's just that my horse has some classes tomorrow afternoon, and I really want to partake." It's my first real lie. I don't actually have any idea what day it is.

"Well, it's unusual to have everything processed that quickly, but I think I can make an exception for you."

I thank him profusely, and hope he knows I mean it.

He is true to his word. The next morning, I am called to the office to begin the arduous process of becoming a free citizen.

My release depends upon my meeting three conditions. First, there must be no weapons in my house. In a deadpan voice, Leslie confirms this over the phone. There aren't even any knives, she insists. I will eat with forks only. Her humor is met with indifference. Apparently, they don't know my brain is a weapon.

Second, I can only be released into the custody of someone

who will be able to keep an eye on me. This really won't be a problem. I don't like to let Leslie out of my sight; it's my default setting.

Finally, I have to make an appointment with a Florida psychiatrist. I try to explain that I don't live in Florida; that I'm going home soon, and I have a regular psychiatrist there. But rules are rules, so I make an appointment. Luckily, there is no rule stating that I can't cancel it, which I immediately do.

When I step foot outside into the bright sunshine and see Leslie, I am flooded with exhaustion, relief, regret, and guilt. The sun hurts my eyes, as if I have lived underground too long. I feel utterly broken.

But I am out. I am with her. Not safe, but for the moment, okay.

Back at the house I shower for forty-five minutes, shave, put on clean clothes, pick up some food, and go to work. It is a fantastic afternoon, akin to a rebirth. I'm experiencing the world with newfound wonder and appreciation.

This lasts until evening. Then everything comes crashing down around me once more, waves of fear and pain washing me into a gulf of desperation with no escape in sight. I am hopeless.

I have come full circle.

2. The Disclosure *Two Years Earlier*

The past is never random, but the real story is now.

It's the dead of winter, and I am packing. Not for myself—that only requires my show clothes, already wrapped in the slippery plastic from the dry cleaner's, and a few jeans and shirts—but for the horses.

This is my life—showing horses. We spend most of the year at our home base in Connecticut, and the winters at the show circuit in Florida. Spring and fall are our off seasons; during the summer, we are on the road, competing in surrounding states.

Gloves are for those who can afford to move slowly in the winter, so my bare hands are icy, but efficient. Each horse—we have ten—has at least one trunk full of equipment. My stick-like fingers make neat stacks of their wardrobes: eight blankets each to accommodate every possible climate condition, leg wraps, boots, saddle pads, earplugs, grooming equipment, soaps, ointments, medications, and supplements, as well as endless selections of bridles, bits, saddles, and every other leather contraption imaginable.

I enjoy the structure of packing, of knowing the animals so well that I can anticipate whatever they might need. The time constraints and the fear of leaving something behind make me sharp. So much of the horses' equipment is customized that forgetting to pack one item can have serious consequences. The importance of coordinating and organizing and multitasking is both stressful and exhilarating.

I'm doing a hundred things at once, and I keep misplacing my pen as I make new lists. My coworkers know to leave me to my own devices. "She's *packing*," they say to anyone who tries to approach me.

The barn where I'm working is large and drafty, an imposing structure of wood and concrete that is wonderfully cool and breezy in the summer, but akin to a freezer in the winter. The horses are bundled up tightly in their stalls, comfortable in their clean knee-deep wood shavings, with huge piles of fresh hay and warmed water.

I put together bags of feed, perhaps twelve different kinds, and calculate how much hay and shavings the horses will need. I arrange for shippers and coordinate move-in dates at the show, factoring in the extra staff needed to load horses and equipment. I supervise the men struggling to stack the five-hundred-pound trunks into the trailer, and make sure nothing is broken or left behind.

The horses need the most preparation of all. Grooming, muscle development, and nutrition are year-round endeavors, but preshow preparation requires its own system for each horse: full-body clipping, trimming every hair imaginable, pulling the mane into a thin, neat line and loosely braiding it so that it learns to grow flat on the right side of the neck. I use every bathing and polishing trick in the book to make our horses look equal to or better than everyone else's. It's a matter of pride. My animals end up sleek, shiny beings, their movements reflecting sunlight as they glide across the ground as smooth as velvet.

It takes me about a month to pack, while also working in my regular barn and riding responsibilities. I ride and show various horses—but June Bug is the one I live for. I shouldn't be her groom and rider, because I don't feel worthy, but I am. It's the opportunity of a lifetime to work with her. A striking bay mare with white socks, she is big and brave and beautiful. She's young and has boatloads of potential.

She's also very expensive. Her owner, Dawn, has several other horses, and won't ride June Bug for many years yet, when the horse is mature and sensible and experienced.

I'm still not sure why I am the chosen one. Perhaps because those around me are generous, caring, willing to offer their trust. I'd like to think it's because I love the horses so much, because I always form close relationships with them, because they always try hard for me. But this is the real world. My actual skills in the saddle are merely fine.

• • • • •

I've worked for Leslie since I started at Vassar—four years of penciling in college classes between my time working with horses, and then an uninterrupted fifteen years since. There was nothing dramatic about the start of our relationship. I don't even remember the first time I talked to her. Our communication evolved gradually, over a period of years, via email.

Email was still relatively exciting two decades ago—at least for us. I'm not sure how long it had been around at that point.

Kids used Instant Messenger, but sometimes the internet didn't work because of a modem or something. We emailed because we could.

It was work-related at first. She started it. And then she continued allowing it. I began slipping in details about my day, and she responded. I elaborated, supplementing the conversation with information about my emotional states, and she kept on validating. I kept on pushing, my correspondence like an interactive diary. She was the cool adult, laid-back, with an "anything-goes" mentality. I didn't pick her as my savior, and she wasn't looking for someone to save. It wasn't a conscious choice. It was who we were, who we still are. I'm a bottomless vat, and she gives and gives.

I kept writing and writing to Leslie. My silly, dark thoughts, my complaints, and my anger had found a receptacle. Then, fifteen years ago, my fingers hesitantly typed:

You know, sometimes I get really upset and then sometimes, I cut myself, like, on purpose, I know that's weird and gross, but it makes me feel better, more in control, I've been doing it since I was thirteen.

And somehow, she responded:

I don't think it's weird, some people drink, I smoke, it's basically the same thing, stuff we do to deal with everyday life, we're all different, but in the end we are all the same.

And I breathed for the first time in my life. The school, my parents, were confused and angry—but Leslie accepted me for who I was. It laid the foundation for me telling her almost everything. And then, eventually, completely everything.

I'm not good with boundaries, and Leslie doesn't have any, so in some ways, she was the perfect mentor for me. In the long run, it didn't set me up for very good relationship skills, but I didn't realize this until much later. I continuously emailed and called, and eventually texted, once that was invented. She is my boss, but over the years, she has also become my best friend and my life coach. And now she is, in my mind, the one person who can fix everything.

A few weeks before we leave for Florida, we have a conversation that will always stay with me. Leslie leans against the side of the barn, smoke from a cigarette curling around her. I can just see her outline from where I'm sitting, slumped on the floor of the center aisle. She's relaxed, like always; comfortable in her existence, at home wherever she is. We're taking a break, watching the sun rise into its own light.

"Can I ask you something?"

"Anything," she says.

I rake my hands back and forth through the dirt. She remains quiet, continuing to gaze out over the paddocks.

"I was just wondering if there's anything you can't handle."

"Sure. But not much." She's not bragging, merely stating a fact.

"Is there anything I could do or say that would shock or surprise you?"

"Surprise, maybe, but not shock."

She turns so she can see me. This is who she has always been— the one who can weather any storm.

I look up. She might be pretty, but I wouldn't know. All I see is someone who is perfect on the inside—someone who has tight brown curls, is athletic in a soft way, and has beautiful hands. I think maybe the hands say it all.

"El," she says pensively, "there's nothing short of you pulling a gun on me or my daughter that would bother me in a significant way."

Her daughter. Always at the forefront.

"So other than direct, intentional harm, there's nothing I can say that will hurt you, make you hate me, or change anything about us?"

"Nothing will change." It's a sentence she's used to repeating. It's this calm confidence I gravitate toward when everything in me is a tangled mess. Even if it means adjusting the truth, she gives me what I need. She gives everyone what they need. It's why we're all drawn to her.

"You might think I'm bad. Horrible," I challenge.

"I won't. I'll understand, whatever it is."

She's forgiven me for so much already. All she asks in return is loyalty. I can feel her presence intensely, a force field of strength, in spite of her looking altogether average in her neat yet unpretentious jeans and sweater. You just never know about people.

But I do know. I remember last week, when I showed her what I did to my arm. She was unfazed. I was relieved—but also wondered, *Shouldn't it affect you?* Is easygoing leniency good, when taken to an extreme?

"It's not what happens; it's how you respond," she says now, not for the first time. "I can handle whatever it is, until you can." She is at peace, which gives her the ability to be tolerant and generous with those who haven't made it that far.

My mind circles back to her hands, refined and lovely and aged by the sun. It is here that I decide to trust in her capacity for benevolence.

• • • • •

I've been going to Florida for the past ten winters. It's a huge amount of work—fourteen-hour days seven days a week—and I feel the weight of being responsible for all of our precious animals so far away from home. But I thrive on the intensity, of competing, of being right in the center of the horse scene.

This year, a strange mix of anxiety and depression has a hold on me. It's not unfamiliar; I've been caught up in periods of depression and self-destruction for a very long time, and though I question whether I am in a good condition to travel, this mental state has never stopped me from doing anything before. I am a master at pushing through.

Still, it's hard to ignore the sinking feeling that washes repetitively over me. So, I do what I always do: email Leslie.

Leslie, I don't know if I can do this. I feel like something bad's happening inside of me. I'm just worried, you know?

El, it's winter, she writes back. It's cold and dark all the time, and you're always nervous before a show. It's normal. You and J.B. are going to do great, just like last year.

June Bug. It always comes down to June Bug, my princess, the privilege that fell into my lap. I want to show her, ride her, be with her more than anything I've ever wanted. It overrides the fear.

So I run. I love to run. Each time my feet hit the ground, my nervous energy is conducted into the earth. And for a short while afterward, the endorphins neutralize the throb of depression at my core.

I run, metaphorically, into the Sunshine State.

• • • • •

Leslie is right, of course. The first few days in Florida are wonderful. The sun lifts my mood as we shed our winter clothing. I spend hours in the saddle, and everything feels right.

The showground is built around an old racetrack. For fun, we slowly canter our horses along it, their interest awakened by doing something other than circling an enclosed arena. The seven show rings are being set up with bright flowers and obstacles for the horses to jump. Tractors grade the footing, and riders try desperately to get their excited horses acclimated to the new environment.

I wander the vast grounds with Michele, one of our head trainers, cooling our horses off as they adjust to the drastic change in climate. We're both in a great mood, filled with expectations for the next month.

Michele is tall, with long black hair. She's beautiful and she knows it. On the other hand, I'm distinctly average, though favorably lightweight and athletic.

Michele has been my trainer since I started working for Leslie. Her teaching style and my learning style are highly compatible: academic, analytic, concrete. I've never been good at trusting my feelings, although I am supremely receptive to those of my horse. Under Michele's guidance, I win, a lot, all across the country.

"Baja shows late tomorrow," she says, "so he can have a quiet morning. Put him in a paddock and then do his bath after that. Dawn's other two go early, so have them ready tonight. Make sure they have their supplements. I called the braider, so that's all set."

"Okay," I say contentedly. I love taking care of my horses. "Will we do some schooling with J.B. before her class?"

"Definitely. I'll let you know what time once I've been to the show office and have the number of entries in each class."

Michele is efficient, all business. She does not want to know about the intermittent darkness of my emotional state. Likewise, I am barred from knowing about hers. I didn't understand this fifteen years ago. How could we work so closely, be in the most intense show environment together, depend on each other, but have no idea what the other is feeling or thinking?

It's about capacity, Leslie wrote once, in response to an email in which I asked those very questions. *Everyone has a different amount and kind. It's not right or wrong or better or worse, just different... when you show, you want Michele at the in-gate, not me... when you want to work through your feelings, you come to me... no one person is going to have it all, that's why we have more than one friend.*

After work is done for the day, I take June Bug out to graze, and feel myself relaxing as we settle into the falling dusk. Maybe everything will be alright.

See? Sometimes you just need a change of scenery, a change in pace, Leslie responds to the upbeat email I send later that night.

• • • • •

Of course, I can't outrun myself for long. The sinking feeling creeps back over the next few days, a heavy weight of pain and destruction and darkness just below my stomach.

"You're doing fine. Focus on J.B.," Leslie encourages. So I do, and it almost works.

Two days later, when I take June Bug out of her stall, I notice that she's limping. Horses go lame all the time, especially competition animals, for infinite reasons, some diagnosable, some not. Sometimes the injury is career-ending; sometimes it requires only a day of rest.

My initial assessment of J.B. is clinical: it's the right front leg, it's noticeable at a walk, and it requires prompt attention from a vet. The emotional aspect is too much for me to process, so I don't.

Leslie and I walk her to the on-site vet. I feel a little numb.

I immediately hate the vet, and I've only laid eyes on him for two seconds. I can't blame him for the fact that we are here, but I can blame him for being male. It's not that I dislike all men, but I need plenty of time to get used to them.

I have no idea whether this vet is any good, but he has a medical degree and I do not. If he fixes June Bug, I'll be willing to forgive his gender. I used to think I was gay, but I'm not. I don't want to be physically intimate with women. I don't want to be physically intimate at all.

I'm distrustful and afraid, and I grip J.B.'s lead rope tightly, as if the vet might try to take her away from me. Leslie could be worried, but she looks calm and relaxed. After all, this kind of thing happens all the time.

The vet is gentle with J.B. He keeps his focus on his work and his phone in his pocket, and his vet techs are cheerful, polite, and efficient. He conducts a thorough examination, including several hours of X-rays, ultrasounds, and tests. He makes no comment throughout, and I respect that he is holding his verdict until he has as much information as possible. I know that in a lot of these cases, no diagnosis is possible. Horses are mysterious, and not very hardy.

When the vet has finished running tests, we gather in his small office to view the results on his computer. The room is neat and organized and smells of fresh wood, with some plaques featuring mildly sexist jokes mounted to the walls. He takes an unreasonable amount of time settling on his stool, opening J.B.'s file, and moving the curser around the page at random, as if he is enjoying holding all the cards. I want Leslie to tell him to quit the theatrics and get to the point, but she waits patiently. I seethe in silence.

"Could be anything," he finally states with dramatic casualness. "Probably an abscess."

This could be great news. An abscess occurs when a tiny particle or bacteria enters the inside of a horse's hoof. It's very painful, but once drained, recovery is more or less instant.

The vet smiles, but the expression doesn't convey the right emotion. Instead of empathy or relief, I read devious amusement.

"Or it could be something more serious," he continues. "There are some abnormalities on the cannon bone. Could be she was born that way and it's nothing. Could be a splint. Or it could be broken."

The fear already circling inside me bubbles. "If it was broken," I state logically, "she couldn't walk."

"Probably not. But it can't be ruled out."

"And if it is broken?"

The vet makes a gun with his fingers and shoots and imaginary bullet, laughing as if he has reached the punch line of a particularly clever joke. "But probably an abscess," he muses.

I turn on my heel and storm out of the office. Pausing to wait for Leslie outside, I hear them speaking casually, and they both laugh. Why is Leslie laughing with him? *Traitor,* I think.

Finally, Leslie comes out.

"What the hell?!" I demand.

"It's okay, El. Think positively," she tells me. "It's probably an abscess."

"And what about the possibility of a broken bone?"

"You know that's unlikely."

"And in that unlikely event, he wants to shoot her?"

"That's a joke, El. Just his manner. He's making fun of your sense of impending doom."

"That is perhaps the worst joke I've ever experienced." His playing on my fear, my vulnerability, generates a violent kind of anger I didn't know I was capable of.

"Yes, perhaps not the best joke, in light of his profession."

"What now?"

"He's going to see if he can find an abscess."

He doesn't—either because it's too deep for him to see, or because the real problem is something else entirely. Even though I am repulsed by his presence, I stand by J.B., tense and quiet. I can feel him mocking me through his slow, exaggerated movements and stupid smirks.

Finally, the vet tells us to put J.B. on stall rest and come back in a few days. He winks at Leslie as we leave, and I want to kill him.

Leslie smiles back flirtatiously, and I roll my eyes at her. But that's who she is—she gets along with everyone. It's an asset in any industry.

I don't want June Bug stuck in her stall all day, but she isn't supposed to move around. I take her outside and sit on a chair, allowing her to stand next to me, absorbing the sun. At first she is restless, yanking on the rope so we can go somewhere. When she realizes that won't be happening, she tries to walk in circles around me, pushing me with her head, pawing at the ground, attempting to bite my arms and the sides of the chair. Eventually she settles down, dozing off in the warmth. One of our clients snaps a picture of both of us sitting quietly and peacefully, our unity radiating. It's the best I can do for her right now.

Apart from moments like this, I move around with a toxic pocket of dread inside me. It takes on a life of its own, becoming existential. A sense of impending doom leans over my shoulder, and I'm unable to ignore it or shake it off.

"You're just that close to June Bug, El," Leslie says later. "You feel for her; you worry for her; you are, in a sense, one unit. If she's not well, neither are you. But she's okay. She's on pain meds. She's perfectly content being lazy and hanging out with you. She isn't worrying about her future; she's living in the moment, and that moment is good. Don't take on more than it is right now."

It makes sense, of course. I like the idea of being that close to my animal. I will protect her, fight for her, live for her. Still, the sinking feeling continues, dragging me to greater depths.

A few days later, Leslie and June Bug drag me back to the vet. I can't stand the thought of seeing him again, but I must.

This time, the abscess has risen toward the surface, and the vet is able to cut it out. I try to feel relief, but I don't.

"This is good," he says, "but we aren't out of the woods. I'm still concerned about what I saw on the X-ray. If she's not sound in a day or two, come back. We still might need to . . ." he makes the gun with his hand again, then looks at me in mock horror. I take a step closer to Leslie.

Playfully, she gives the doctor a shove. "Can you stop messing with her like that?" she says, laughing.

"It's so easy! But fine. Can I mess with you instead?"

"All day long, assuming my vet bills disappear," Leslie jokes. I feel as if the vet is touching me, even though he isn't. Still, the feeling is repulsive, dirty.

"Leslie," I implore once we are headed back, "this is all so wrong!"

"Not really. He's a good vet; you just don't like his personality. I'm not saying I do, but I meet people on their terms. It helps. He found the abscess, right? That's what matters."

Two days later, J.B. is still lame, and we are forced to confront the X-ray findings.

"I'm going to fly in our vet from home," Leslie decides. "He knows this horse. He has her old X-rays from her pre-purchase exam. I think this is best." I want to hug her. Finally, someone is coming to help June Bug—and me.

Our vet comes on the first flight available, and quietly sets up his equipment in J.B.'s stall. I want to thank him, tell him how happy I am to see him; but the words suffocate. I almost don't care what he finds. I want the truth. I want Bug and I to be safe. It's been reduced to that.

An hour later, the vet states that J.B.'s bone defect shows no changes in comparison to her old X-rays. It's insignificant—probably congenital. He believes the reason for her ongoing lameness is the depth of the abscess, and that it will take longer to heal than normal. She won't be rideable for the rest of our stay in Florida, but she will be able to graze and go for walks, and eventually make a full recovery.

I am endlessly relieved and grateful, but it's not enough to shut out the pain inside me. I remain sitting in the shavings in J.B.'s stall, leaning against the tent fabric because standing requires too much of me. Irrelevantly, it's my birthday.

That evening, I take June Bug for a walk in the soft air of dusk. It's wonderful out, a warm breeze gradually sifting through the layers of the night.

After a while, I try to lead J.B. back to her stall, but she plants her feet. I give her ten more minutes, gazing contentedly across the grounds while she roots around in the dirt with her nose. She still doesn't want to come in, and while I could make her, I don't. It's too right, the two of us out under the comforting glow of the moon, speaking through our silent connection. We aren't alone—a horse show never sleeps—but a curtain has been drawn over the frenzy of the day.

"I'll stay out here as long as you'd like," I tell J.B. "I promise, I'll protect you from the world."

• • • • •

I expect to be able to let go of the concern and fear and discomfort now that we know June Bug will be fine, but this is not what happens. It's as if the whole situation nudged me off the top of a steep hill, and now that I'm sliding, I only gain more and more speed in the descent. I am increasingly afraid—terrified, even. Discomfort morphs into sharp pain and dread, and there is no escape. The pain is psychological, but it manifests as a stabbing sensation at my core.

I keep asking Leslie what's wrong with me. I ride around the showground looking for answers. I start running again. It helps at first. Our rental house backs onto a nature preserve, and I run along the dirt-packed trails leading in and out of the woods. Around every corner, there is a surprise—a magnificent lake with sleepy pelicans, a meadow flanked with trees dripping in Spanish moss. It's so much nicer than trudging along the shoulder of the straight streets back home, alternately being sprayed with sticky road salt and squishing through dirty patches of snow. I look for happiness here in Florida; I really do.

I get back to the rental after a run and feel a fraction better, but as soon as I lie down, exhausted, I'm suddenly wide awake. One night, in the early hours of morning, I wander onto the porch seeking a change in scenery. To my surprise, Michele is there too, smoking and staring into nothingness. We don't acknowledge each other, perhaps because we know we are both running from our demons, too immersed in our own conditions to reach out—two people wanting to feel safe, or not wanting to feel anything at all.

The mornings offer a slight reprieve. Usually I have one or two coworkers with me, but we are understaffed this year, so Leslie gets up early to help me prepare the barn and the horses for the start of the day. It's a special gift—I get an hour or two of alone time with her, which is highly unusual amid the demands she seeks to fulfill around the clock. I treasure the time like water in the desert. I start arriving even earlier so that we finish the morning chores early, leaving us a little free time before the clients arrive and the day really starts.

It becomes our sacred ritual: sitting on trunks, drinking coffee, and watching the show come to life. It sustains me through my pain. I still hurt, sitting there, but it's the only place I want to be, if I have to *be* at all.

During this time, for perhaps the first time in our relationship, I ask Leslie about herself. I have a good feel for her values and beliefs, of what frightens her and what keeps her going, but it's different to hear them verbalized.

I'm in perpetual awe of her undying optimism. "How do I become like you? You're the most confident person I know."

"I don't think I'm any different from others. I guess I just believe that if you know right from wrong and work hard, the right choices avail themselves."

"I do, for the most part."

"You do. Now, stay focused on the big picture. You're surrounded by supportive people, great horses, and a rewarding job. Right now you're depressed, but it won't always be like that, because you have the right foundation."

"You make it sound so simple."

"A lot becomes clear if you're able to put aside the small stuff. It's something I work on, myself. It's not always easy."

"But sometimes bad things happen. Things go really wrong."

"Of course. But mostly there's a solution, if you take a minute to run all the possibilities through your head. Then you just pick the best one."

I am riveted, not so much by the content of Leslie's conversation, but by the impressions I receive while sitting and hearing her speak—the sound of her voice, her cadence, her interminable calm.

"I get why everyone is drawn to you," I state softly.

"I don't think people are drawn to me. But I'm interested in people. I love to hear about their paths, their goals, their ambitions. And I believe everyone has something to offer, whether it's big or small."

"I'm too selfish for that."

"No, you just have to learn that you too have something to offer, and that it's worth sharing."

But all I feel now is how much everything hurts.

"What do you think is the most important thing in life?" I ask.

Leslie pauses for a moment, gazing into the distance. I see the silhouettes of horses moving about the grounds.

"A sense of accomplishment—whether it's achieving a small goal, or something big, like providing for Lena."

Of course. Lena, Leslie's daughter, is her reason for everything. Even when it's just me and Leslie, Lena is still with us.

I feel the beginning of anger, but it sinks into resignation—and then rises in defiance. After all, I'm the one who is here now, and Lena is still sleeping. I fought my way into Leslie's life; Lena was born into it. I feel terrible for being glad Leslie is divorced.

"I value integrity, loyalty, and hard work," Leslie continues. I wonder how we can be so similar, yet so different.

Then it's time for Leslie to leave me, to get on with her day, to help the rest of the world. Despite her grounding presence, I feel worse each day. I am poison. But I'm also a fighter, and I fight.

After a long, hot day, I decide I will go for a run—but not a normal one. This time I will run until the pains stops, until I exhaust it into oblivion. I don't care how long it takes. If I keep feeling, I will keep going.

I run into the setting sun, through dusk and into darkness. When I can no longer see through the trees, I make my way onto the sleeping streets, shadowy under the road lamps. My determination is my adrenaline, but I am human. After about fifteen miles, numbness begins its descent. I head for the rental house, slowing to a walk in the driveway. My legs are jelly, my head slightly dizzy, but I think I have won. It shouldn't take this much, but at least I have succeeded. Still in my running clothes, I sink onto my bed and close my eyes.

And there it is. The pain. In my stomach, seeping into my arms and legs and head. I don't know what's worse—its return only moments after I spent three hours killing it, or the horror that I am this powerless. Incredible.

I try to sleep, but it's elusive.

Leslie, what do I do? I can't anymore.

Apparently, no one sleeps, because at 4:00 a.m., she answers, like an omnipresent god.

You can. You put one foot in front of the other. That's all you can do, and it will be enough.

Then Lena gets sick. Just a cold at first—then, suddenly, pneumonia. A dampness falls over all of us. Lena is a good part of the reason we make this trip, so she can gain experience competing at a national level. She's missing school, and Leslie works tirelessly to give her this opportunity. These things happen to every athlete, but that doesn't make it easier.

At seventeen, Lena is highly intelligent and emotionally perceptive, with many of Leslie's qualities: kindness, rationality, empathy. It makes it impossible to dislike her—and anyway, how can I dislike what's most important to Leslie?

But Lena relies on Leslie to even greater extremes than I do, and her sudden illness comes as a shock. Everyone is subdued, and Leslie is distracted. She spends only a short time with me in the mornings, and on some days, she chooses to stay at the house altogether. I understand, of course—what kind of person would she be if she didn't?

Still, practically, it's detrimental to me. And I can't complain, because I'm not the one who is sick. I envy Lena's tangible symptoms. What kind of person does that make me?

One evening, I go for short run. Even though it is no cure, I still appreciate the few minutes between arriving at the house and the return of the pain. When I come back, I drag myself through the living room on the way to the shower—and that's when it happens. Something major by virtue of its insignificance.

Leslie is on the couch. So is Lena. It's very simple. Lena is curled up, asleep in Leslie's arms. They both look so perfect, so content, despite the circumstances. It's a picture that burns. That's all it is.

It is as if a train has hit me head-on. It's that physical. Feeling nothing and everything, I calmly continue on my way to the shower. I lock the door and pop the blade out of my razor—something I've done a thousand times before.

I do not cut deeply, because there is no cut deep enough to touch this. I settle for the action, the ritual, because it's all I have.

Still in a sort of trance, I enter my room and fall on the bed. I text Leslie. *I need you.*

And she comes, closes the door behind her, and sits on the carpeted floor.

"What's going on?"

"I cut."

"You do all the time. Why now?"

"I can't tell you."

"Stitches?"

"No."

"Why can't you tell me?"

"It's too embarrassing."

She is silent for a moment, then shifts into a different position. "When you came into the living room. I know."

"You do?"

"I know you pretty well. And it's okay."

I half smile, sheepish and relieved, glad she doesn't spell it out. Leslie gets up. "You know where to find me."

She leaves, and I fall back on the bed and try to figure out how I ended up this pathetic.

It does not get better. During the day, obligation forces me onward, but during the night, I have nothing.

I try to stay in bed, but I can't. Without distractions it's just me and the pain, and we don't want to be alone with each other. There's a gym in the clubhouse of the gated community where our rental house is located, which is open twenty-four hours a day. It's a beautiful facility, empty almost every time I go. The fluorescent lights and buzzing ceiling fans are my comfort in the night. In solitude, I use the cardio and weight machines, do sit-ups and push-ups on the mats. Eventually, I exhaust myself and lie sprawled out on the floor, the darkness pushing in through the windows.

When I get cold, I wander into the locker room, which looks like a place where wealthy people might socialize. There are lotions and soaps and thick warmed towels, and booths for hair-styling or makeup. I try out all the soaps as something to do, but mainly I sit on the bench under the shower and cut. Dark red water pools under my feet. I am in my own universe, but there's an odd sort of comfort here.

· · · · ·

"I was thinking something," Leslie says one evening. I perk up. "It could be crazy, though. I don't know if I should say anything."

"*I'm* crazy," I remind her.

She smiles. "I'm afraid that if I'm wrong, it might be offensive."

This is unusual. Leslie never wavers. She's always so sure of herself.

"I want to hear anything you have to say, if there's even a chance it might help. And I don't think you'd hurt me, even unintentionally." I'm convinced.

Leslie nods and suggests we go for a walk, which is also unusual. This is not something she ever has time for during a show.

We set out along the nearby golf course. It's lovely outside, the sun just low enough to be gentle, a light breeze rustling the trees. We wind our way along manicured paths lined with tiny flowers, side by side with me half a step behind. I will follow her forever.

"I could be way off, alright?" she hedges.

"You usually aren't."

"Okay. It occurred to me when we were at the vet. Just a weird theory. You distrust men, you've struggled with emotional regulation since I've known you, and you can be very self-destructive. And there's the pain you experience all the time. I wonder, a long time ago, if a man did something to you. Something mean, and you've never really recovered. I'm sorry if this is out of place; it's just the feeling I get."

Everything inside me freezes. Then heat rushes through me like an eruption of hot lava, liquefying my insides. All I experience is a pulsing sensation. Sound and vision blur. I don't know how my body is still walking when I feel so far, far away from it.

I hear my voice in the distance. "It's not . . . it's not way off." Why do I even say this? I'm not me. I have no concept of time.

Leslie is silent, although I know she is there. We keep walking, briskly but not fast.

Slowly I start reconnecting to myself. Shapes come into focus, and I regain sensations through a lingering numbness. It's not unpleasant. Maybe we could keep walking forever in a world where nothing is real and nothing hurts, because I'm with her.

Leslie starts talking about something trivial, and we arrive back at the house. I get in the car to go back to the show to check on the horses for the night, then stop at the grocery store on the way home. Under the fluorescent lights, I find myself staring dumbly at the selection of food. I don't know how to choose. I still haven't quite returned to this world. The pain is still with me, but its edges are blurred.

Leslie understands. Leslie knows more than I ever will, even though neither of us have any facts. A hand has been extended to me through the darkness. I could live like this, I think.

I leave the store without buying anything.

• • • • •

The conversation with Leslie sustains me for a day or two. When the pain threatens, I think of the secret only Leslie and I share, and a warmth envelops me.

Alas, nothing is ever simple, and it is merely a brief reprieve, during which the pain is marshaling its forces. Depression and anxiety merge to form a lethal combination, and it comes alive in a new way, like electricity ceaselessly shooting back and forth. Cutting and exercising are no longer useful tools.

I stop sleeping completely, which causes a frenzied, otherworldly delirium.

I spend the nights wildly emailing Leslie. It helps push time forward, and is my only bridge between appearance and reality. Not much of a sleeper herself, Leslie patiently writes back in the only language we have. *It will get better. You are not alone. Keep fighting.*

It's dark in my room, but I actually see black, as if I'm generating the lack of color. I taste and touch and feel it. I hear it, too, a deafening roar coming from within. It's an endless warped carnival ride. I wish for death, but intuitively know that I am meant to live.

Just when I think I've felt it all, a new feeling surfaces. It's disgusting, revolting, the most disturbing of all. And surprising. I've never really felt it before, but I know what it is. It's sexual.

I leap off the bed. I must escape by any means. The golf course spreads before me in a three-dimensional canvas. I blindly scramble along the narrow paths that wind though soft dips and rises, and scurry beneath a circle of massive trees huddled in dripping moss, a fairy-tale world of danger and beauty. It is here that I lie down and stare up at the stars, the cold, wet ground reaching into me, and come to a decision. It's a decision that can only be made subconsciously.

When the stars fade, I go to the horse show. I have robotically finished the morning chores when Leslie arrives.

"Let's go for a drive," I demand. She doesn't say anything, just nods casually and retraces her steps to the car.

"Where to?"

Anywhere. She'd drive me anywhere. "Doesn't matter. Just drive."

She backs out of the parking spot. The last thing I see before I close my eyes and curl tightly into a ball is her manicured hand shifting the car into drive. The passenger seat belt does not sound an alarm at my unbuckled self. Perhaps it knows to leave me alone—or doesn't think I'm really there.

"I want to tell you."

"You can tell me anything."

"But it's like, bad."

"That's fine."

"You won't be able to look at me ever again."

"I don't believe that will be the case."

"It's going to change everything."

"Only if you want it to, or let it. It won't change anything for me, about us."

"But it's gross. Embarrassing."

"Remember, I've told you there's nothing I can't handle, unless you pull a gun on Lena or me."

"I'm probably not going to do that." I try to make light of the situation, but my humor falls flat.

"Then we're good, whatever you want to say."

I am comprised only of nerve endings. We are silent for a minute, my tension and fear raging against Leslie's calm and confidence.

"It wasn't rape." This seems like a good way to start. "It was just, he touched me, and

I hated it, but maybe I didn't, and I held my breath until it was over. It was over a period of time. I don't know who. A man. It was a very long time ago." I am shaking uncontrollably, sweat pouring down my body, although I am not sure if that's due to nerves or just because the seat heater is on. It's hard to breathe, and I am too small for the magnitude of what I feel.

"El. I don't mean to minimize this in any way, at all, whatsoever. But I had a general idea of what you were going to say. And I had prepared myself for something far worse. I'm not saying it wasn't terrible, but it's manageable in terms of us. It's not too much for me to handle, and you have nothing to worry about. It's time to start understanding that you're safe now."

If I could have reached up into the sky and asked the gods for the perfect response to my revelation, this is what would have been sent down. Is she a god?

When I feel the car stop moving, I open my eyes, but stay drawn into myself. We are back at the show. I can't move, can't be left alone. I'm not ready. Leslie knows this.

"Leslie?" Her silence gives me the space to move on. "It's not just that this bad thing happened. It made me bad."

"No, it made you *feel* bad. There's a big difference."

"I see the difference, but it's both. You know why? Because sometimes—more than sometimes—I wish it would happen again. That's bad. That's on me."

"That seems perfectly logical to me. It's your inner child attempting to control a situation in which you had none. You're hoping for a different outcome. You seek control."

I feel this to be true, but how can she know? Can she really see past the monster I am?

The first emotion I manage to single out is a violent surge of gratitude. Empowered, I keep going.

"A few days ago, when you were with Lena on the couch, I was upset because it wasn't me who was sick."

"I know. I understood right away. There's nothing wrong with wanting to be taken care of when you're hurt, but the first step is trusting the people around you to be able to do so. You have a lot of good people in your life. Allow them to help. If it feels safest, start with me. I care; I can listen. You're not broken. You just need to relearn, and it's not too late, not with the right environment."

I am stunned speechless, almost thoughtless. Leslie really is a mind reader.

"Your adamant rejection and fear of any human contact? It's contact that you want. It just became too dangerous. I'm not saying you should go around hugging everyone. But change is possible. It's possible to unravel who you've become from everything that hurts so much."

The tension has melted into a new state that is soaked with relief. Nothing is okay, everything is okay, and I am awed by the understanding and compassion I have found. I'm not sure where my shoes are.

A sudden thought occurs to me, of a foreign shape and texture. "Leslie? You really believe me, don't you?"

"Of course. Why wouldn't I?"

"I didn't think anyone ever would." I spoke. She listened. She believed. She heard. A broken sequence put back together.

"You believe me." I need to hear myself say it again. Tears threaten to fall, but don't. I have been stunned into paralysis. "Do you think I'll always be this attached to you?" I wonder.

"For now, but not forever. You are going to redevelop, like a child might, the way you perhaps didn't when you were young. You'll stay attached until you don't need to be."

I can't imagine ever getting there, but I am riveted by how much senses this makes. "And you believe me?"

"I believe you." I could listen to her say this forever. "I have to go pick up Michele from the house now. You need to move ahead with your day."

"But I can't! How could I?" I have no idea how to function in a world that has been turned inside out. How can I interact with clients? How can I pretend everything is the same?

"Of course you can. You didn't forget how to do your job, or how to ride. Just go in there and put one foot in front of the other."

I do. I locate my shoes and wobble across the parking lot. When I get inside, I furtively look around, but nothing has changed. No one is staring at me. How can everything be normal when so much has changed?

I lay out the tack and start preparing the first horse to show.

Somehow, the day passes. When I arrive home for the evening, I dump my belongings in my bedroom and wander into the kitchen in search of food. I'm too tired for the gym, and I spend a moment leaning against the counter, disoriented.

This is when it hits me. I freeze, and then slowly, quietly, as if afraid to tip the balance, make the assessment. It can't be true— but it is. For the first time ever, the pain inside me is gone. Not eclipsed or suspended or overshadowed, but *gone.*

I creep back to my room, awed and a little afraid. It's incomprehensible. Miraculous. Feeling without pain.

From now on, I write to Leslie, whatever happens, for as long as I live, I will send you one email each night, and all it will say is "Thank You." I will thank you for the rest of my life.

And to this day, I do.

• • • • •

I fall asleep, and stay asleep until it's time to get up. Upon rising, I realize I am the most tired I've ever been in my entire life. But as I push through the foggy sludge, one truth emerges: the pain is still gone. Nothing else matters.

The show will last only a few more days. I ride, with moderate success, and revel in the delight of my new state. I join the others for dinner instead of hiding in the solitude of the gym. I talk, not about myself for a change, but about books and foreign countries, surprised that I actually have something to say. I no longer begrudge Lena her illness. At night I experience nothing, because I'm asleep.

A couple of hours before my flight home to Connecticut, a client takes us to lunch at a fancy restaurant. We sit in the shade under an umbrella and enjoy the warm breeze. Michele and I engage in a lively conversation about intelligence in elephants. I have stepped outside of myself and into the world, and the world receives me with open arms. If last week I were asked to describe a world without pain, I couldn't have.

Later, I'm sitting at the gate waiting for my plane, and all of a sudden, completely out of the blue, I start to cry. I am shocked. I have no idea why it's happening, and I'm terrified of losing my newfound reality. I call Leslie, panicked.

"Don't worry. You're just afraid that the feelings won't transfer to your life back home. Your mind is expecting a return to the state in which you left. It's not going to be like that. This is who you are now. It doesn't matter where you are geographically. And remember, I'll be there, too. It's been an emotional month."

How does she have the right answer for everything? My tears keep falling, but they have turned into tears of relief. I board the plane, and for the entire flight, tears run slowly down my face. It doesn't matter what others think. If anyone comments, I will just smile. But no one does.

The next six weeks are surreal. Part of me knows that this is a type of honeymoon, that no one can be this happy all the time. Yet I cannot deny the magnitude of the transformation. I feel weightless. Walking is easy; I'm gliding along without having to support myself. Working is easy. Everything takes no effort whatsoever. I wonder if I should wean myself off my antidepressant medication. Maybe I was never really depressed at all.

I write to Leslie, perhaps even more often now.

I didn't know it was possible, this kind of connection to another human being. It opens up another dimension, another universe.

Anything is possible. But not everyone can communicate like we can.

I talked to a cashier today. About NOTHING! But it was fine. It didn't suck the life out of me. It just happened. I am now a person who can speak.

See the things you are capable of!

What I feel the most is love, directed everywhere, but mostly toward you. Is that weird?

It's not weird. It's opened up new feelings, new options.

I can envision a FUTURE! It's like there is HOPE. I am SAFE. Is this what normal people feel like?

I think this is your own journey.

Is this me now? Or was the person I used to be me?

It's all you. This is you fulfilling your potential.

All this positivity might be sickening if I wasn't so damn happy. And I'm going to appreciate every trite second of it, because to me it is real, and that's all it needs to be.

For a nonbeliever, it is a profoundly religious experience. I understand the feeling, if not the logic, of people who have faith in miracles. It makes me want to fall to my knees and worship, believe in something supernatural, give my existence to a higher power, for no greater joy can be found. Leslie has become my god. She is the one who took away the pain, led me toward salvation.

I get a tattoo. It's an abstract design of a heart, a symbol of gratitude to commemorate what Leslie has given me.

• • • • •

Back home in Connecticut, we return to our usual routines. When I spend time with Leslie, I try to listen to who she is.

We sit on the edge of an empty flower bed outside the barn. The snow is trying to melt, a discussion between winter and spring. Leslie is smoking, and I'm absorbing her presence. I drag my foot back and forth through a trickle of water and watch her hands, touched by the Florida sun, delicate and pretty, but capable of work.

She tells me about her life: her incredible parents who clawed their way out of poverty, her subsequent fear of being poor. Her affinity for numbers, which landed her a prestigious accounting job, until she gave that up to run a bar, and then to own a gym. And always horses throughout, until it became only horses forever. The hardest thing for her was her divorce, but now she likes the independence.

It's difficult to imagine that Leslie belongs to so many people, and none at all. She is the behind-the-scenes hero, helping everyone but never losing her sense of self; the unassuming character who doesn't sweep in with a Superman cape and a cloud of dust behind her, but takes one quiet step at a time, believing that if you take enough of those steps, success will come within reach. I'm not the first person she has helped, I won't be the last, and I am certainly not the most important. Part of me wants everyone to know who she is, and part of me wants her to be my secret.

There has been nothing fake or imagined about these last six weeks. It's real happiness, but unfortunately, it's also the calm before the storm.

It's very gradual. At first, I try to pretend the clouds aren't rolling in, but I can't hide when the first raindrops fall. Some evenings, I burst into tears for no reason. Leslie tells me this is normal, that it's safe to feel now. I believe her, and then I'm fine for a while—until it happens again. The tears are acceptable—but slowly, the pain comes creeping back as well. I ignore it, reason with it, relabel it, sit with it. I don't want to admit to myself or to Leslie that it is back. But eventually, I'm no longer able to deny it. Not only has the pain returned, it is back with a new force and power that completely knocks me off my feet. I have let myself down; I have let Leslie down; I am so bad that nothing will ever help. It's pain plus complete hopelessness.

And this time, I know there will be no second miracle.

3. The Boot Camp

I have a therapist, Sheila, whom I've been seeing on and off for many years. It was Leslie who suggested I start making those appointments, a long time ago.

When I first met Sheila, I knew we would get along well the minute I met her dog. As soon as I walked through the door to the office, the dog scampered up the stairs and threw herself at my feet, a wiggly tricolored little mutt. Grinning manically, I bent down and hugged her.

"I see you've met Annie," Sheila said, smiling, when she came through the door into the waiting room. A tall lady, she had blond hair and blue eyes. "She likes to come to work with me. I take it you won't mind?"

Reluctantly, I got off the floor to greet Annie's human properly.

Our first session went adequately. Sheila was smart and intuitive. I knew therapy wasn't going to change my life, but I also knew someone like me should have a therapist. She got bonus points for not demanding I stop cutting, because she said it was a symptom, not a problem in itself. In return, I refrained from questioning her interior design skills. Everything, absolutely everything in her office was purple.

Sheila taught me the importance of being able to sit with the pain. She taught me that everything is a process. Sometimes, she said, it's not about making the pain go away, but about waiting it out. That means and progressing blindly, knowing that even backward movement, or periods spent without moving at all, are a necessary part of the journey.

Significantly, Sheila was also the first to ask the question, long before even Leslie did.

"El, do you have any history of sexual abuse?"

"No," I told her wistfully—wistfully, because I wished my problems could be that easily explained.

"It doesn't have to take a traditional form. You might not even realize that's what it was. You might have no clear memory of it."

"I understand, but still, no. Trust me, I've considered it. It's a dead end. If there was something, I would tell you. I know it's your job to ask."

"That's true, but I also see other signs. You distrust men. You report no desire to have any kind of physical relationship. You have detailed your aversion to any type of human contact, and you are surrounded by animals more or less constantly."

"I like animals," I said defensively. "Liking animals isn't indicative of having been abused."

"You're right, it's not. It's just that some people work with animals as a coping mechanism. That's why animals are often used in therapy. They offer patients a safe way to interact."

"That's not entirely the case for me."

"I accept that. But you do have an extensive and complex history of cutting. I see that a lot in trauma patients."

"But by no means in all of them."

"Certainly not. But do you see a theme in the books you read? The things you write about?"

"Yes, because the fallout of sexual abuse is a complex, interesting topic. If I liked to read about war, it wouldn't mean I'd been in one."

"No. It's just a lot pointing in the same direction."

"Possibly, but it's missing the central piece: that nothing actually happened."

"I think there's a strong possibility something did."

"That's because you're a therapist. Believe me, it would almost be a relief. I'm not being difficult; I'm not in denial. It just isn't the case."

"Okay. We'll move on."

And that was that.

Did she plant the seed, or merely shed light on it, allowing it to sprout and grow?

• • • • •

There is still a trace of doubt, a question in my mind as to whether I fabricated what Leslie wanted, or expected, to hear. Even though I've frequently entertained the idea, I have no concrete evidence. In the end, I choose to believe that I told the truth to the best of my ability. It feels right.

• • • • •

We've been back from Florida a few weeks. I'm in the barn, grooming Leslie's favorite pony, a fat, lovable, talented little monster named Patriot. It's Saturday, so people are milling about: children wishing they could be me (spending all day with horses!), and their parents following behind, fervently hoping their offsprings' obsession is just a phase. When they look at me, I wonder whether they see someone too simple-minded for a real job, or someone who graduated top of her class, someone confident enough to follow her dreams.

I'm both—and someone else entirely.

As I efficiently polish off the last of the mud in which Patriot chose to roll, I realize that something is seriously wrong. It's a new development amid the array of my previously acquired dysfunctions, a sort of fatigue—a passive feeling that I don't really want to live anymore. So far, it seems far away and hollow, meaningless apart from its novelty. I want to do something about it, though.

Leslie, I write. *I'm tired—not like I need to rest, but like I need more space to process everything that happened in Florida. Like it's too much just to get on with life as usual.*

Whatever you need, baby, I'll support you.

I research. Even between riding and caring for the horses, I do internet searches on my phone. It gives me strength, knowing that I'm actively planning for change. I look into outpatient programs and ranches far away in Montana, that promise healing among mountain streams and horses with flowing manes. I almost fall for it—six months of being someone else. But I have a whole barn of horses here, with neatly trimmed manes and immaculate coats. How much of a difference would a change in altitude really make?

I don't feel capable of functioning in the free world. I want to be hospitalized. However, that seems unnecessary, as for all intents and purposes, I'm functioning just fine in spite of the way I feel. In the end, I come up with a compromise.

Leslie, I think the only way to achieve what I need to is to design my own program. I am determined and motivated enough for this to work. I want to take two weeks off and process all the stuff that's in my head, in a very structured way.

No one could do that better than you! she writes back.

So I start to plan. I will spend the two weeks in North Carolina, just south of the Blue Ridge Mountains, in the glass house my parents own. I buy three notebooks to devote to the three periods into which I intend to divide each of my days. The first will focus on dialectical behavioral therapy, a widely used system I've found helpful in the past. It focuses on techniques for regulating emotions, tolerating distress, practicing mindfulness, and increasing interpersonal effectiveness. I order the official manual, which comes with lectures and examples and practice exercises. The second period will involve relaxation, physical activity, and interaction. I plan to enjoy nature, sit by the pool (sitting still is a skill I want to acquire), run, hike, bike, and engage in meaningful conversation with my parents. The last period I will devote to reading and writing on topics I deem relevant to my mental health. To help with this, I buy some psychology books. Knowledge is power.

I've never left June Bug before, and I feel guilty for leaving my pet bunnies (who always stay home in Connecticut) so soon after returning from Florida, but I tell myself there can be no gain without sacrifice. I have to find a way to live that doesn't hurt so much.

Given the Florida disclosure, I decide that Sheila should also be included in the plan to reconstruct my life, even though I haven't talked to her in years. I call her and schedule some phone sessions for the two weeks I'll be gone. It makes sense to include an actual doctor in my self-designed program.

"It's not a bad idea," she says when I tell her what I've decided. "You might get a lot out of it, probably more than you would from the more garden-variety programs out there. There's a book you might be interested in reading as part of your experience. It's called *The Body Keeps the Score*." I make a note to order it.

"Once last thing," she goes on. "I truly believe this is a great idea for you. Your commitment and intelligence will take you far. But doing this alone will have its limitations. Recovery isn't a solitary process. There's a human element your plan is lacking."

That's fine. I have no interest in such an element. I only need Leslie—but for the two weeks I'm away, I will cut myself off from her. I want to learn to help myself without relying on her.

The evening before I leave, I have dinner at Leslie's house. When it's time to say goodbye, I dissolve into tears. She hugs me, and it's the first time ever that I don't want to spontaneously combust after being hugged.

"You'll be amazing," she says, but I'm not sure I know what she means. "I'm proud of you. And I'll be right here when you get back."

I know she means it, but what I can't explain to her is that I have no sense of object permanence. Kids grasp this concept around age two—if Mom leaves the room, Mom can still exist. But to me, out of sight means out of existence. Mentally, I'm not even two.

It takes a lot for me to leave work. That isn't something you do in my profession; if you do, you're weak. Jen, our manager, gives me the time off, but judgment radiates from her.

Jen is tough—not like the loud whirlwind of Michele's personality, or the quiet cement Leslie is made of. Attractive but self-conscious, she stays well behind the scenes. Sometimes when it's just me and her, she talks about her own problems with anxiety. She loves the horses, to the extent that she's able to do hard things like put the overweight animals on diets for their own good or confine an injured horse when it desperately wants to go outside and play in the paddock. She understands the sometimes-tough dynamics of working with show horses, balancing the importance of winning with their well-being. Perspective is her strength. She's my go-to for figuring out how to look at a situation objectively, for understanding how to do the right thing. We both care about our animals too much.

As I'm leaving, her voice in my head says, *I don't care that you're severely depressed, or if both your legs are broken. Come to work and do your job.* It's my voice, too. The horses come first. But I can also imagine her saying, *I respect you enough to expect the best of you. You're part of the elite, the ones who are strong.*

• • • • •

I'm afraid, but my mind is made up. As soon as I get to the airport, I pull out my iPad and start making lists and goals and allot space in my notebook for continuous documentation of what I'm feeling. This proves somewhat futile, because I quickly realize that I feel every possible feeling at all times. The only difference is the order in which I rank them.

My dad picks me up, and on the way to the house, I try to tell him a little about my plans. I even ask him about his brother, who is schizophrenic. He is receptive, but the contrast between us makes me feel awkward. Here is a man who used to run the world. I can barely make it through an hour without falling apart.

Both my parents are retired. They live in an award-winning house they designed themselves—a modern marvel of glass and steel, imposing by virtue of its unpretentious union with the landscape it was built into. It's in a small town in rural North Carolina. To balance out the country life, my parents also own a traditional weekend home in the city of Charleston. I'm so proud of their success. It gives me hope that somewhere in my genes is the potential for me to do something right.

I unpack my few belongings in a room with a view of the lake and the Blue Ridge Mountains behind it, and immediately make use of the infinity pool. I don't really swim, but I figure splashing back and forth will be good exercise. My parents are avid athletes. At least I inherited that.

I plant myself at the kitchen table with my materials spread out before me and decide to start with DBT—dialectical behavioral therapy. I read the manual I bought, I take notes, I memorize passages. I try to understand what comes naturally to most young children: how to be aware of what I'm thinking and feeling, how to communicate and regulate emotion, how to walk myself away from trouble. I appreciate that the goal of this therapy isn't to eliminate painful emotions, but to reduce the suffering they cause. I love the idea of letting thoughts and feelings pass through me like waves in the ocean, and here at my parents' house, there is plenty of opportunity to practice.

I sit still and allow myself to feel my pain in its full scope and magnitude. Instead of trying control it, I give it space to splash around and pass through me, in the hope of loosening the trapped tension. It doesn't really help, but at least the theory makes sense, both physically and emotionally. I know that mastery is often a matter of practice and perseverance. I believe change is possible.

During breaks in my studies, I work on a photographic documentary showcasing the different types of lizards and geckos that sun on the warm tiles around the pool and eat bugs off plants. It is an activity involving creativity, luck, patience, and novelty, and I find it exciting and rewarding. I spend hours editing the pictures, ensuring the beauty of the lizards' little bodies is captured in color and light.

"Can you tell me what you are working on?" my mother asks tentatively as I scrunch over my notes in fierce concentration. She is, as always, caring and concerned, but careful not to invade my privacy.

"Techniques for processing feelings more constructively," I venture. I want to share; I want to let her in, but I know I am too much, in every sense. I talk to Leslie because, as much as she cares, I can't hurt her the way I could hurt my parents. And what kind of monster would I be if I did that? They are loving and supportive and present. As a child, I received what I needed emotionally and practically, in the context of appropriate rules and structure. I had a little brother to play with, and a few good friends. I was allowed a guinea pig and a puppy—the highlights of my childhood—and given the opportunity to do chores in exchange for riding lessons. My parents led by example, teaching me the values of hard work and kindness and integrity. I didn't eat school lunches—my mom made me my favorite sandwiches with lots of pickles, and my dad patiently spent long evenings explaining to me over and over again that two plus two was never going to equal anything other than four. He was the successful engineer, she the stay-at-home mom. I can't spell "engineer" without using the autosuggest feature in Microsoft Word.

So when my mother asks what I'm working on, what can I say? That I need a book to teach me how to be a normal human, and that my greatest ambition is to get through the day without some phantom pain killing me? I'm not going to risk implying that she failed, and I am too embarrassed to suggest that I did so when I was raised in such favorable circumstances. I am so incredibly grateful that my brother is now a successful businessman, happily married with a house of his own. His success shows that the problem is with me, not my parents. And the thing is, they don't love me any less. So I do what I can. I protect them from my dark side.

Unfortunately, that doesn't always leave much else to talk about.

•••••

I order the book Sheila recommended, but as an ebook. Because of the format, I can only see individual pages presented in order, so I have little to no way of knowing what the book as a whole entails. I can't easily highlight or backtrack, so I decide to take copious handwritten notes instead, and assign myself forty pages a day.

Bessel van der Kolk is a psychologist who focuses his research on how trauma—loosely defined—affects the organism as a whole in aspects of development, attachment, and neurobiology. It's natural that Sheila would suggest such reading, but it does sound interesting, and after my disclosure to Leslie in Florida, it may even be relevant.

The book starts powerfully, detailing how certain experiences can cause physiological changes in organisms, resulting in the recalibration of their alert systems. He explains that traumatic experiences cause an organism to produce increased levels of stress hormones and change the ways they filter information, which may make it difficult for them to learn from everyday experiences. These stress hormones overreact quickly, and are slow to return to baseline. A huge amount of energy is needed to suppress this inner chaos, which, after trauma, can becomes a type of default setting.

I am riveted. Intellectually, this is fascinating. And I feel exactly this way. Sure, it's easy to project oneself onto any psychological profile, like reading a horoscope—but this very much seems like me. It is such an accurate way to describe how I feel, with words I can understand and process. As I read this book, not only do I see myself in an abstract sense, but every cell in my body comes to life, like lights on a Christmas tree. It is a deeply visceral sensation, a series of tiny explosions that feel surprisingly pleasant.

There has always been something absurdly off about me, something crazy and irrational, and that's somehow become who I am. The frantic panic surrounding Leslie's every departure, the inability to understand that out of sight is not the same as out of existence, the notion that every minor departure from the norm is nothing less than a five-alarm fire.

Recalibration. That is exactly what I need. I must be reset, like a frozen computer. I know how I'm supposed to feel and think and act. If I am recalibrated, I might actually be able to do it.

So much depth in the first dozen pages. I keep reading:

"We now know that their behaviors are not the result of moral failings or signs of lack of willpower or bad character—they are caused by actual changes in the brain."

I almost burst into tears. All the times I've berated myself, felt inferior, believed I am fundamentally flawed, and tried to compensate through sheer willpower—all the times I reworked my principles and values—all the times it hasn't been enough— all those times, and Bessel van der Kolk says it is not my fault. I don't know him, and he doesn't know me, but we speak.

Each page is like unwrapping an unexpected gift.

"When we try to help people with faulty neuroception, the great challenge is finding ways to reset their physiology, so that their survival mechanisms stop working against them. This means helping them to respond appropriately to danger but, even more, to recover the capacity to experience safety, relaxation, and true reciprocity."

Safety. My word, my mission, the gaping cavity in my soul. Relaxation is a lost cause, though it would be nice if my relationship with Leslie was more reciprocal, more about *us* than *me*. But safety is my Holy Grail. I will consume this book, find Bessel, kneel before him, and beg him to show me the way.

"Traumatized people are often afraid of feeling. . . . [T]heir own physical sensations . . . are the enemy. . . . Change begins when we learn to 'own' our emotional brains. That means learning to observe and tolerate the heartbreaking and gut-wrenching sensations that register misery and humiliation. Only after learning to bear what is going on inside can we start to befriend, rather than obliterate, the emotions that keep our [internal] maps fixed and immutable."

How can he know this is how I feel? More importantly, how can I meet his demands? My new sense of intrigue is refreshing.

Later, my mom and I sit in the car on the way to grocery store.

"What's the book you've been reading?" She really wants to be part of my life.

"It's . . . well." I try to think on my feet. She knows I've entertained the idea of sexual abuse, because on a particularly brave day long ago, I asked her whether anything of that nature had ever happened to me. She was confused and said no, and it felt authentic. We are a family of terrible liars.

After that, I never mentioned it again. This might be the most insulting thing one could say to a parent: You didn't keep me safe. And in my case, it doesn't feel right. Growing up, I *was* safe. But somehow, that changed. There are so many contradictions.

In response to my mother's question about the book, I say, "Well, it's sort of about brain chemistry and learning pathways. About how and why we become who we are."

I'm not sure I could have made my response any vaguer, but she takes what I give her. "And how do you think you became how you are?" she asks.

"I'm still working on that."

"I wish I could help. I can tell you that you didn't really like anyone but Dad and I for a long time. You wouldn't let anyone else hold you, and you refused to go to preschool or on playdates."

Interesting. Perhaps this is simply who I am—I was born weird, and nothing made me this way. But the book.

This is as far as we can both go.

• • • • •

On the days I get excited about the book, I can run faster, longer. With each foot hitting the concrete, I feel a type of energy being released, and I imagine the pain being drawn from me like poison and absorbed into the junglelike vegetation that hugs the cliffs on the side of the road. I see it washing away in the streams trickling from boulders, flowing into the muddy, stagnant waters of the reservoirs. I keep running, hoping to leave it behind. The soft mountains loom high and majestic around me, and I try to find a place for myself in this world. I try to *recalibrate*—whatever that means.

I feel inspired, but alone. I desperately want to share my findings with someone—preferably Leslie—but I'm determined not to break my self-imposed rules. I wonder if this is what Sheila meant, by a "human element." The desire to reach out to Leslie pulls like a rubber band stretching too tightly inside me, and I try to breathe through the tension so it doesn't snap. I made a commitment. Two weeks without Leslie, so I can learn to be more independent.

I'm not sure if I'm trying to torture or comfort myself, but sometimes I imagine Leslie walking around the barn, feeding carrots to her favorite horses at the end of a long day. There is something touchingly innocent about it. In my mind, she looks like a little child holding her hand out, in awe of these large creatures with soft lips gently reaching for treats. The image makes me love her, and reminds me that we all started out as that child.

• • • • •

I call Sheila, but her parents are visiting and she cannot talk.

A surge of irrational anger floods through me. First she makes me read this book, and then she leaves me alone with its consequences. I'm pretty sure she told me she wouldn't be available throughout the whole two-week period, but right now, I can't focus beyond my own needs.

So what, I think rebelliously. I can do it on my own. I have the willpower. I turn back to the book. It's too powerful to walk away from.

"... *[T]rauma almost invariably involves not being seen, not being mirrored, and not being taken into account. Treatment needs to reactivate the capacity to safely mirror, and be mirrored, by others...*"

It is uncanny that this man understands my internal state so well. I am drawn to Leslie because she is my mirror. She validates how I feel, tells me those feelings are real and that therefore, I am not crazy. She allows me to mirror, *safely*. It is through her that I dare to look at who I am.

Each page hits closer and closer to home. When Bessel begins to write about attachment, I see myself dissolving like a melting pile of ice. I think I might cry, but it's too overwhelming.

"*Our attachment bonds are our greatest protection against threat.* ... *Traumatized human beings recover in the constant of relationships* ... *The role of those relationships is to provide physical and emotional safety, including safety from feeling shamed, admonished, or judged, and to bolster the courage to tolerate, face, and process the reality of what has happened.*"

It is uncanny. I crave normalcy like others crave food and sleep and sunlight. Bessel says what I feel is normal—and that other people have felt it before, so much so that it merits a book's worth of words. My irrational attachment is not irrational. I need this relationship with Leslie to keep me safe. It's okay that I can't do it on my own. Bessel says so.

I must, beyond a shadow of a doubt, show Leslie this quote right now, so she understands. I already know she understands, but here is scientific proof—though of what, I'm not quite sure. To show her my craziness directed toward her is acceptable? To thank her for being the only person who can ward off danger for me?

All I know is that I must email Leslie. Due to the gravity of the circumstance, an exception must be made. If I don't, I'll implode, and I won't be able to continue my studies. After all, Leslie's role in my life is to reduce my tension.

To save face, I ask her not to respond. That way I won't become distracted awaiting her reply.

• • • • •

I keep studying psychology texts. Keep taking notes. In a text called *Attachment in Psychotherapy* by David J. Wallin, I read this passage:

". . . [P]atients who would be described as preoccupied with the attachment figure's availability...behave as if they are hopeless, both about relieving distress on their own or about the possibility of engaging help without making their distress overwhelmingly obvious to others. . ."

Thoughts tumble through my mind. Leslie's availability. Can't relieve distress without her. *Making it overwhelmingly obvious:* cutting; insane emailing; every thought amplified to maximum pitch and volume; frantically believing that if I don't scream, I won't be heard. Completely incapable of managing my internal state. If these mental states are specific yet common enough to be documented by medical professionals, that must mean there are doctors out there working toward a resolution.

· · · · ·

Finally, Sheila reappears.

"How's it going?"

"Great!"

"I'm glad. I'm proud of your progress."

"That book—it's amazing! It's me, every step of the way. But now I'm not sure what to do about it. How do I not feel this way?"

"You keep following the path. You keep reading. You allow the process to guide you. Remember, it won't be straightforward, and it won't be the same for everyone."

I'm not sure this is an answer, but it's not as if I expected a crisp solution in three sentences. The book says I've been this way for so long, my reactions and emotions have become a fixed pattern of neural pathways. I know I can't undo a lifetime of faulty wiring in two weeks.

"There's another book you might find meaningful. It's about attachment theory."

Because I'm spinning on an exciting but disorganized intellectual carousel, I decide to download this new book and have a look at it, and then come back to Bessel. I'm a starving person presented with a huge buffet, and I don't know what to eat first.

In this other book, *Patterns of Attachment: A Psychological Study of the Strange Situation*, author Mary Ainsworth finds that young children fall roughly into three patterns of attachment. She gauges which of the three patterns a child falls into by placing the child and his or her caregiver in a room. Those children who exhibit a secure attachment style explore the room freely, using the caregiver as a secure base from which to venture out. Having this base on hand helps to foster their confidence. When the caregiver is removed, the child becomes upset; but when the caregiver returns, the child is immediately placated and continues to explore.

Those children who exhibit an avoidant attachment pattern do little exploring whether or not the caregiver is present, and show little affect upon the caregiver's departure or return. Based on measurements of the children's heart rates, this indifference is a protective mask for distress. This type of child has openly suffered severe abuse, and has almost no expectation that their caregiver can provide any safety.

I am hugely relieved not to see myself in this latter category. I may be dysfunctional, but I have always believed hope and salvation exist. I was never ignored or neglected.

There is a third category of children: those who exhibit an ambivalent attachment style. In this third situation, the child is anxious from the start that their caregiver might depart, and remains distressed when the caregiver returns. The children who exhibit this type of behavior seem to believe that displays of anger or helplessness will aid in controlling the situation by preventing the caregiver's departure in the first place.

Both the avoidant and ambivalent patterns of attachment, I learn, are considered insecure attachment styles.

I smile to myself. After so much reading, I feel I have little energy for any additional prophetic self-discoveries, and I merely take comfort in the fact that there exists a place for me. Whether I was born this way or became this way, it's a definable problem with, ostensibly, a definable solution.

And then, out of nowhere, rage and indignation hit me, rising like fire licking through walls. *Why were the caregivers taken away from the third set of children? Who approved this study? Why was such torture inflicted on them intentionally?* And at the same time, I want to scream at those stupid children. *Be like the first set of kids! Of course the caregiver is coming back, you idiots! It's all your fault for not being normal!*

The comfort of finding myself in these pages battles with the fear of what I am learning, and now it's Sheila's fault for giving me this hideous book. I need to stop reading it immediately.

But I can't help but wonder how someone with such a secure upbringing as mine could possibly develop attachment problems. I have had plenty of practice with change. I was born in Boston before we moved to Canada, and from there to Germany, then to California, and then to Connecticut. Within Germany, we moved several times. New schools, new languages, new friends, new horses, and I never had any problems. We vacationed with family in Spain and England, and travelled across much of Europe. We lived in the countryside and in big cities. My dad went to Harvard, and my mom taught drama and French. I speak several languages. I am the last person on earth who should have an attachment problem.

I want Leslie.

I return to the first book, and learn about Bessel van der Kolk's model of internal leadership. He breaks the mind down into three semiautonomous functioning modules. Each module has a different role in protecting the self. The "managers" are the rational parts of the brain; they are in charge and tell the other modules how to behave. The "exiles" are the brain's toxic waste dump. They contain difficult memories, sensations, and beliefs, and make themselves known through overwhelming negative emotions. Finally, the "firefighters" will do anything to make emotional pain go away, even if this means destroying the entire building in an effort to put out the flames. They are creative and devious, constantly trying to find a way to protect the rest of the modules, as well as themselves, from pain. It doesn't matter how they accomplish their goal; in the quest for safety, anything is justified.

I feel a surge of empathy, guilt, and comfort. My firefighters work so hard on my behalf. Sometimes the only way they can get the pain to stop is by telling me to cut. My exiles are too loud, and my managers are useless. Suddenly I see beauty, not in the sun and clouds playing hide-and-seek upon the mountains, but in the determination and ferocity of my battle.

Bessel goes on to say that in order to achieve integration and peace, each of the brain's modules must be acknowledged. I take his words very literally, and focus separately on each module, writing down whatever comes to mind as I do. I listen. I write until there is not a thought left inside me.

I wonder how long it will take until it makes a difference.

· · · · ·

I'm lying on the stone wall outside, talking to Sheila over the phone.

"I think what you're doing is exceptional. I don't know many who have your drive and determination to get better. You're going to benefit immensely. Just remember, healing is a process.

It won't be finished once you get back home."

"I don't expect that. I've been this way for a long time. I know it's going to take a while to undo, but I'm hoping I now have some of the tools and information I need."

"Exactly."

"It was intense, finding myself so completely in that book."

"You were ready. Leslie allowed you to feel safe enough to be receptive. You weren't ready when I first met you."

"And you were right. Something did happen. It must have. I feel it in every way. I just wish I had more information, you know? Is it strange that I don't? Will I ever?"

"It's unusual for people to recall traumatic memories once they are blocked, but not impossible. As to whether you'll learn specifics, the jury is still out. Keep an open mind. Listen to yourself."

I've been listening so hard to myself that all I hear at this point are echoes. Nevertheless, I thank Sheila before hanging up. Then I push myself off the wall and walk slowly back toward the house.

In the evening, I spend time with my parents. We watch TV so we can be together, but not in a way that forces conversation. I love them so much, and I think that is why I find talking to them so difficult.

"You're making progress? Is it going to help once you get back home?" my mother asks hopefully.

"Yes; and I think so," I say, because it's true.

"You know we'll support you no matter what, right?"

I do know that. I couldn't ask for anything more.

My dad isn't much of a talker, but I feel his presence. He is at home in his own empire. His story is a classic one: rags to riches. To him, the world outside didn't matter then, and it doesn't matter now. I get my radical perseverance from him, only without the results. He's too kind to be disappointed in me, but I'm not.

I might enjoy this time I spend with my parents, but the pain is seeping into my legs, distracting and overwhelming. I wish I could stay in the semidarkness with them, watching *Shark Tank,* but I need to be unconscious, so I claim fatigue and head to bed.

•••••

The next day, I push on. The take-home message from my reading is that I can't ignore, fight, or run from the pain. It's not random; it means something, it is an adaptive response. The pain is my "firefighter" module trying to get my attention, to protect me.

This isn't self-help—it's science. The vagus nerve connects the brain to the inner organs. I am not crazy for feeling psychological pain in such a physical way. The pain is a type of energy produced by the brain stem, and it must be titrated slowly. Another wonderful word, titration. Recalibration. The pain is released through registering emotions as physical experiences, trusting and befriending the messages they send, and identifying contrasting feelings associated with relaxation to act as a counterpoint. The goal is to decrease the reactivity of the nervous system, take it out of overdrive, and allow its normal responses to restore themselves. Mindfulness and deep breathing can activate emotional regulation by decreasing the activity of the amygdala and its physical triggers. We can tolerate more if we become aware of the interplay between our thoughts and sensations, and understand that both thought and sensation can be transient instead of fixed. In the end, it is safety, at a visceral level, that allows for recovery.

Everything circles back to attachment, and how the bonds we develop with others create a foundation for recovery. As I've always believed, everything comes back to Leslie.

The text suggests that a close relationship with a therapist can provide the context to relearn secure attachment, recalibrate the nervous system, begin to titrate the pain. I want to believe it, but I don't. Sheila is a good therapist, probably a great one. But she isn't part of my everyday life in the way Leslie is. Maybe Leslie doesn't have the clinical training, but she is safe, and it all comes down to that.

My brain is spinning from all these discoveries. The extent to which I can identify with these concrete concepts is intoxicating. Now I need to put them into action.

The pain is always worse in the evenings, so I start there. To establish a better relationship with the pain, I break it into three separate entities and assign each a name. I befriend Lucy first, my most frequent companion; she is the dull ubiquitous throbbing just under my lower ribs. McKayla appears when the pain starts getting worse. She is Lucy's outer ring, moving up into my chest and down into my gut. Sam means business, radiating into my arms and legs, stopping around the elbows and knees.

I speak to them as they appear. Sometimes it's only Lucy, sometimes all three. I speak to them even if they lie dormant. I don't try to summon them or push them away. I try to give them the voices they demand. I apologize for trying to silence them, for calling them useless and evil, for hating them so intensely. I try to listen. They don't use words, so I allow myself to feel their texture and consistency, their quality and depth. I see their colors and listen to the frequency of their pitch. I taste them, and tell myself this is all for the best. I present them with a blank canvas, an empty page, an onstage solo, and open myself up to the performance. I credit myself for solid work and berate myself for expecting radical change.

• • • • •

It is my last weekend with my parents, and I have completed the work I set out to do. I want to spend the last two days relaxing and preparing myself for reintegration. Unfortunately, time stops. There is no way to bridge the gap between now and going home. The lizards no longer hold my attention.

The problem is animals. Never in my life have I gone this long without touching, communicating, or interacting with them. My skin feels naked. My insides are simply gone. I'm an empty husk. My cells vibrate in desperation. I have no problem with the human language, but it doesn't reach as deeply into me. Sheila was right. Animals are safe. They stop me from missing what I'm incapable of having otherwise.

Except with Leslie, of course. She is my connection to humanity. I've gone nearly two weeks without her, and I'm not letting my resolve weaken so close to the end.

I look up the address of a nearby wolf sanctuary online, and dutifully my mother drives me hours through the winding forest roads of the mountains, pretending this is a fun adventure—or perhaps simply happy we are doing something together. When I see the wolves, I feel calmer. I focus on all the characteristics I am so familiar with—the fluid movement of their limbs, their intercommunication, the rippling colors of their coats—all these small things I take for granted when working with animals, only now understanding how their world has sustained me. I even love the creatures few others do, like spiders and snakes and strange bugs. But with the wolves, there is no tactile element, and the calm disappears as soon as we begin the journey home.

I think of my bunnies, back in Connecticut, and need them desperately. My experience with bunnies started as one of the best things in my life, but then turned on me viciously. There is one thing I try not to talk about. I wanted something cute and cuddly—something that was mine in the way the horses I ride and care for never can be, an extension of myself. I went to the pet store and bought Jinx, a miniature gray-and-white bunny.

Rabbits give you what you give them. They can have no personality, or way too much. Jinx loved going to work with me. He'd ride on my shoulder like a parrot while I drove. (People still hate me for driving five miles per hour the entire way.) At the barn, he stretched out on the windowsills, relaxing in the sun. If it was cold, he ran laps in an empty stall like a racecar. At home, he rearranged my room to his liking. He pushed things around so he could jump from the floor to the chair, from the chair to the table, from the table to the dresser, and from the dresser to the top of the shelf, whence he surveyed his kingdom. He was happiness embodied. He loved me unconditionally. I fed him whatever he wanted, which was everything. One day, I woke up and he was dead.

The vet suggested it was because he was eating too little hay and pellets, and too much "candy," like fruits and rabbit treats. I'll never know for sure, but I think I killed the love of my life. The End.

To survive my guilt over the loss of Jinx, I ran to the store and bought the first bunny I saw. I needed a redo, even though I didn't deserve one.

Riley was Jinx's opposite. Shy and reserved, he refused to come to work with me, hiding under the bed when it was time to leave. He slept under things, not on things, and far away from me. He got carsick.

Eventually, though, Riley and I came to love each other deeply, indescribably. It's wrong, but I force myself to block out what I did to Jinx, because some things are too horrible to be compatible with continued existence. To love as thoroughly as I do, to feel so much responsibility, is both a curse and a blessing.

• • • • •

I become a little irrational. On the final day of my stay in North Carolina, I decide I may be able to make it through if I focus on food. Food has always been my friend, because amid all my dysfunction, I have a wonderfully healthy relationship with it.

I decide that my family will go to brunch, the best of meals; and it will be perfect. I spend considerable time searching for the right place, reading reviews, studying menus. Nothing is one hundred percent right. I demand that my parents call their friends for recommendations, and then I overanalyze their suggestions. Finally, the hours creep into darkness, and still I have not found what I am looking for. I am losing my mind.

Eventually, I fall asleep.

My parents stay up late into the night, finally finding a place that meets every one of my arbitrary yet crucial criteria. It is indeed perfect, the sun sparkling off the lake outside my window seat, the food of exactly the right proportions and quality. There is some satisfaction in the notion that if I try hard enough and have the appropriate help, I can make something work.

I don't deserve my parents—my mom, who quietly persevered until the child version of myself sat euphoric in the back seat of the car, cuddling a fluffy white puppy named Sky. My dad, who taught himself computer science over eight consecutive hours so he could successfully retrieve the term paper my computer deleted—irretrievably, the experts said. I enjoy this morning with them.

The last night should be easy, the conclusion of an overall successful trip. I am only one sleep and a flight away from my home and animals and Leslie.

Inexplicably, however, the pain skyrockets. I try to practice my newly acquired skills, talk to the pain by name, accept what it means, and open myself to communication. But it's too loud; it doesn't respond to its names, and I can't process through the shrieking volume. It is instinctually impossible to accept such searing discomfort. Even my eyeballs hurt. Perhaps I should call that pain Eileen.

I get into my parents' marble shower and try to relax under the pressure of the powerful stream of water. Crying is something Sheila taught me about a while ago. She says the endorphins released when people cry are very similar to those I evoke through cutting, and that allowing and even encouraging myself to cry will scale back my desire to cut without losing the psychological benefits. I was never a big crier, so it took almost a year of work, but gradually I came to agree with Sheila.

Now I cry because nothing I do can make the pain stop; because I haven't hugged an animal in two weeks; because Leslie is so far away I don't know her anymore; because I have parents who move heaven and earth for me, and still nothing, absolutely nothing, is ever enough.

· · · · ·

Relief washes over me as my plane hits the runway, though I know I won't trust the reality that I am back home until I physically see everything I've missed. The joy of touching my animals and interacting with Leslie, who seems genuinely happy to see me, sustains me for several weeks. Perhaps the work I did in North Carolina did make a difference. If nothing else, I have a new appreciation for all the good there is in my everyday life.

I am surprised to see that in only two weeks of being away, I have missed autumn in New England. When I left, the leaves were still green, a few red dots cresting their edges. I am sad that the red has now given way to brown. In a few days, the crumbling leaves will sink to the ground.

· · · · ·

After Florida, North Carolina, and an old undercurrent of omnipresent suspicions, I believe I am on the right path, at least in terms of processing the elusive shadows of sexual abuse that flicker over my life. I don't need concrete evidence of that abuse; my symptoms in the present are proof enough.

But if you keep walking the same path, it will eventually wear down. Does this prove it was the right one—or have you simply made it so?

4. The Triathlon

I don't make rash decisions, so my newest idea is well thought out, planned, and researched. Only then do I go public with it.

"But El, you can't really swim."

"You don't have a bike. And where are you going to go on any fifty-mile bike rides?"

"It's twenty degrees out. You think you can just walk into the ocean?"

"You'll need a trainer. There are techniques, strategies, rules to follow to prevent injury."

"Your knees will never hold up."

"If you want to do a triathlon, great, but how about starting with a small race, instead of one that's so absurdly long?"

El, if anyone can do this, it's you.

• • • • •

Everyone asks me why. The answer is because I need a focus, a goal. Because I love working out, and I love pushing myself. Because I want the world to know I'm not pathetic.

This is what I say. It's the truth, but it's far from the whole truth. It comes down to the fact that I am weak. North Carolina gave me the space and the information to allow me to deal with the pain, learn how to manage it, live with it, and reduce it. Yet I was not strong enough to overcome it. Now it's time to play to my strengths. I will become so physically strong, nothing else will matter. I will become an endurance athlete, because I am capable of enduring. I will exercise so much that my brain will be flooded with endorphins and depression won't stand a chance.

I've faced the implications of any possible repressed trauma in my past, and now it's time to move forward.

I'm not normal, so my newest goal cannot be normal, either. I want something challenging—but I also need to be able to continue working full-time and traveling to horse shows. I can afford to spend some money to achieve my goal, but not a vast sum. I fall in love with the idea of competing in a triathlon. Three accomplishments in one, proving that I am three times as strong. When I come across the Ironman Triathlon, I know I've struck gold. I will compete in this race, and in doing so, I will become an Ironman, a bionic being. I will transcend flesh and become metal.

I pick the Ironman 70.3, which is half the distance of a full Ironman, but still intense: 1.2 miles of swimming followed by 56 miles on the bike, followed by a 13.2-mile run. The race must be completed in eight hours and thirty minutes. An Olympic triathlon is less than half this total distance. I register for an event to be held in the foothills of the Catskill Mountains.

I print out the recommended training program. It calls for nine workouts a week—three each of swimming, running, and biking, with one day off. The program gives suggestions for each workout's length and intensity, eventually building up to six hours for the longest one each week. I can't imagine doing this, but what I stand to gain is motivation enough. When the winter show season rolls around, I still manage to fit in training around fourteen-hour workdays. In over a year of training, I never miss a single session.

Once everyone around me realizes I'm serious, they are extremely supportive. My coworkers let me leave work a few minutes early so I can fit in another workout. Michele starts bringing me extra food. One of our clients helps by gifting me a gym membership. My parents call every day to offer advice and encouragement. Leslie is Leslie. I become tired, hungry, overwhelmed, frustrated, and bored, but all the adjectives in the world can't hold their own against my motivation and commitment. It isn't hard. It simply *is*.

Brick. Refueling. T1 and T2. Splits. Aero bars. Century. Intervals. Race packet. Transition bag. Aid station. Gels. Taper. Drafting. Age grouper. Base metabolic rate. Anaerobic threshold. This becomes my language.

I research the equipment triathletes use. I talk to people, nodding in agreement when I don't understand their words, and running home afterward to look them up online. I count calories to make sure I'm not losing weight. I learn about how and what to eat during my workouts. I watch videos; I read about what to do during the all-important transition from the swim to the bike, and the bike to the run. As is the case for any beginner, the more I learn, the less I feel I know. The amount of material I need to absorb is overwhelming. But every time I feel the impossibility of my success creeping into my thoughts, I look at the Ironman logo. It's all I need. It's a complete lifestyle change. That's what I love about it.

• • • • •

First things first. Triathlons always start with the swim, presumably so competitors aren't as tired when they get in the water and are therefore less likely to drown.

Confidently, I stride toward the gym's indoor pool in flip-flops, towel over my shoulder as if I am a real swimmer about to work out. From the shallow end, I casually start down a few steps into the water, then abruptly stop. Icy.

I take a breath and turn to the lifeguard. "What's the water temperature?" I ask, as if making conversation.

She rolls her eyes and smiles. "Eighty-four."

I nod. That doesn't sound bad.

"I know," she continues. "Way too warm for a real swim, but we run classes for senior citizens every day, so it has to be that warm."

I sigh in acknowledgment and find new resolve. If a ninety-year-old woman can paddle around in here, I should be able to swim a few laps.

Ironically, the hardest part of this entire pursuit is not the monumental effort and time it requires, nor the loneliness of the three-hour runs, nor the monotony of the endless white lines on the side of the road. Nor is it the fatigue, nor the constant sense of failure. It's the cold. In the pool, in the ocean, on the bike. Even during my runs, cold sweat clings to me.

The water is foreign, touching me everywhere, sloppy and invasive. I can do a sort of breaststroke-paddle from one end of the pool to the other, as long as I stay close to the edge so that I can hang onto it during breaks. I persevere, and eventually manage to swim one length without having to touch the bottom.

"You've certainly been here a lot in the past few weeks," the lifeguard comments. She's skinny and pretty and around my age, with hair that stays straight in spite of the humidity.

"I know," I say proudly. "I'm training for an Ironman." In hindsight, I must have seemed delusional.

"You know, you'll have to learn how to swim freestyle," my mother tells me later.

"No, breaststroke seems easier. I can keep my head above water."

"It won't be fast enough, or sustainable over a mile. And you'll be the only one not swimming freestyle." My mother swam competitively in high school, with some degree of success. I seem not to have inherited the gene. To me, "freestyle" sounds like you can do whatever you want, but apparently it refers to the front crawl.

Nevertheless, I start practicing freestyle—and find it a ridiculously futile process. I manage about three strokes before sinking. I hate my head being underwater, and I can't figure out the sideways breathing. I swallow huge amounts of chlorinated pool water. The cold liquid trickles into my brain through my ears. Not everything is possible for everyone.

When it happens, it's like the moment everyone remembers from childhood, when you are suddenly riding a bike without training wheels. One minute I'm flailing around—and the next, I'm suddenly moving forward in an awkward but self-sustaining rhythm. It's magic.

Three months later, I can swim a mile in about an hour. That's very slow, but the sense of accomplishment is huge. The smell of chlorine becomes the smell of success.

Still, I remain nervous about my pace. I need to be sure I'm able to make the cutoff time so that I can proceed to the bike. I know swimming in the open water of a lake or an ocean will be very different from swimming in a pool. I won't have the benefit of pushing off a wall after a lap. There will be currents, waves, and tons of people splashing around me. I know someday I will need to practice outside, but right now, the snow and ice are my excuses.

I'm frustrated that the water doesn't let me go faster. It's too thick; there is too much friction. I watch professionals online and try to mimic the way they glide. I try so hard that my muscles feel weak and jellylike when I get out of the pool. Dry land rejects me after the water. I can't imagine biking and running after a workout like this.

I never end up being a good swimmer, though I do develop a love-hate relationship with swimming. With my earplugs and goggles and swim cap, I experience a type of relaxation in the deafening quiet of the water. I'm in my own world, the weightless movement a little like flying. On good days, the water allows me through, carries me. We work together. The sensations are so unlike any I am used to, and that's nice.

One day I arrive at the gym and the pool heater is broken. Only one or two men are pounding out a quick swim. I don't want to join them, but there is no choice. I can't miss a workout.

Getting into the pool is an exercise of its own, one that requires placing mind over matter. A million needles pierce my flesh, each movement prompting a new rush of pain and torment.

"Kinda exhilarating, isn't it?" the man in the next lane says with a grin. I try to say *No, not really,* but my mouth and jaw are stuck. It hurts so much, but I know pain.

I finish my hour, then stand under the hot shower in the changing room. I make the water as hot as it will go, and yet, I'm still freezing.

Wearing all my outdoor clothes, I get on the treadmill, yet throughout my next hour of exercise, I remain cold and numb. Time to call it a day.

When I get in the car, I blast the heater. Driving home, I become disoriented and pull over, dizzy and confused. I'm not sure where I am, even though I take this route every day. Maybe it's the heater—perhaps I'm too hot.

The next thing I know, I am home and crawling into bed under a million covers. I'm so cold, I feel sick. I fall asleep.

I wake up many hours later, feeling normal, if hungry. As I prepare a large meal of protein and carbohydrates, I look up the symptoms of hypothermia. Seems I've just had my first brush with it.

This could be problematic. My event is next spring, which means the lake won't have had the benefit of soaking up summer heat. Worse still, the lake is fed by snow runoff from the mountains.

I look into other triathlons scheduled for August in Arizona, but they ultimately prove unrealistic for me. My horse show schedule is inflexible.

The race's guidelines permit the use of wetsuits when the temperature falls below a certain threshold, and I look into ones meant for far colder temperatures than I will experience. I hear wetsuits increase buoyancy, but I also need to able to move. I do some calculations, but don't like the answers. I buy a suit anyway.

I read about people swimming the English Channel, and

experiments that have been done to increase cold-water tolerance in humans. The results are not encouraging, but it seems ridiculous to concede defeat due to my inability to tolerate the cold.

Once the weather turns favorable, I decide it's time for the open water, and to test the wetsuit. My friend Charlotte and I drive to the local beach after work. It's not a particularly nice beach: a half mile of dirty sand covered in strings of seaweed rolled up by waves that bubble in thin layers of slime. Even though it's a weeknight, families are having dinner on concrete tables along the boardwalk, and mothers are dozing on colorful towels while their children shriek and splash in the shallow water. Young couples argue, and elderly couples walk slowly, hand in hand. I feel ridiculously out of place in my wetsuit, swim cap, and goggles.

Charlotte snaps a photo of me walking away knee deep into the water. In the photo, my head is turned toward the camera, and I have a pained grin on my face. The lighting is perfect—the sun setting, the water a deep blue. It's beautiful, even if I look as though I'm heading to my execution.

I love the picture. To this day, it reminds me of the unlikelihood of what I can do.

Saltwater tastes even worse than chlorinated pool water, and because of the waves, drawing a successful breath when I turn my head is hit-or-miss. I literally eat bubbles of pollution. Every time something slimy touches me, I cringe. I hate not being able to see the bottom, even though I know I could touch it if I needed to. I stay so far in toward the shoreline that I rip open my hands when I rotate my arms, scraping my fingers on the rocky seabed. But I make the right movements, and don't sink, although I realize I'm not actually making any forward progress.

"You're done already?" Charlotte asks when I emerge fifteen minutes later.

"I am so done. Take me home."

"Okay. You did great," she says tentatively. I am the most pathetic athlete in the world.

"I'll come back next week."

Much later, during my last open-water practice, I swim back and forth along the half-mile strip of beach with relative ease. I've learned how to sight, which is to glance forward every ten strokes or so to make sure I'm still swimming in a straight line. The pool has a line to follow on the bottom, but the lake will not. I feel joy and excitement, and I have not died from swallowing poison. I'm sure all the sunbathers would be impressed, if they weren't fast asleep.

I don't often feel depressed while swimming, since there's so much else going on from a sensory perspective—not to mention the constant undercurrent of exhaustion and fear. I have managed to acquire a whole new skill, and that's rewarding. Still, I don't enjoy it.

· · · · ·

The bike is slightly easier.

I had a mountain bike as a child. Now I am fitted for a sleek road bike, and I buy the right shoes, a helmet, extra tubes, a pump, and basic tools. I love the bike's gray frame, and it's so light I can carry it up the stairs to my apartment over my shoulder with one hand, which makes me feel professional and strong.

It's amazing how, if you work hard enough at creating a persona, it can actually become real. So far, the biggest thing I've learned from this experience is that you don't need to *do* any-thing specifically monumental to achieve something monumen-tal—you just need to let a lot of smaller actions add up.

My first ride around the driveway is wobbly, but not terribly difficult. I learn to use the gears, and due to my natural caution and the excellent sense of balance I've developed while riding horses, I never crash or fall off.

I go on my first long ride on the road, come home exhausted and sore, and laugh at the idea of being able to run after this. I can hardly walk. I look at the fancy gadget attached to the han-dlebars and am dismayed to find that I have cycled exactly five miles. To make the cutoff time, I will need to complete the fif-ty-six miles in four hours and twenty minutes.

Once again, the problem is the cold. Even temperatures that sound reasonable, like the forties, fifties, and sixties, are not so for me. Each morning, I set out wearing layer upon layer of sweaters and pants, gloves, with a hat shoved under my helmet. I look ridiculous on my competition bike, and I know I will even-tually need to wear only a triathlon suit. It's usually early when I begin—still dark and freezing until the sun rises and warms me. Then I'm stuck overheating in my winter jacket, and I sweat so much that I become cold all over again. On one occasion, irritated, I start shedding layers as I ride, tossing them onto the curb, and retrace my route afterward in the car to retrieve them all.

During the bike leg, refueling will be essential, and I begin to practice this during my workouts as well. Every fifteen min-utes, I ingest fluid, gel, an energy bar, or some other form of protein. Triathletes experiment to find out what works best for them, and some tolerate a greater intake than others. Finally, something I am good at. I am able to eat almost anything while working out. I don't think the idea is to eat a three-course meal, but I do. Food is stored in the built-in pockets of my trisuit, or taped to the handlebars of my bike. My bike is a Christmas tree decorated with food ornaments. I'm aware that I look like a lunatic—a deranged bag lady bundled up and eating breakfast on an expensive road bike.

"How was the ride on Monday?" Leslie asks at one point.

"Not good. I got a flat. For the first time. I tried to fix it on the road, but I couldn't."

"So what did you do?"

"Walked home carrying the bike. I didn't want to damage the rim of the wheel."

"How far were you from home?"

"Eight miles."

"El, why on earth didn't you call me?"

"I don't know."

At home, it takes me three hours to fix the flat. I could have taken it to a bike shop, but I am too stubborn.

I don't live in an area that is conducive to biking. The constant up-and-down of the hills makes me worry that I might not be able to ride on flat ground when the time comes, and the roads are heavily traveled, with massive potholes every few feet. Most drivers will wait until it's safe to pass me, but more than once, I feel a car brush my arm as it blows by. I'm sure I make people late for work, contributing to the general decline of the economy.

Forget the swim and the run for now. I need to be able to bike fifty-six consecutive miles. Even though the official workout program calls for fewer miles to start, I want to know if I can manage the full distance. I get to forty miles on sheer will-power, but my knees hurt so much, even I can see that if I don't stop, I'll ruin them for good. I berate myself for trying to do too much too soon and wonder once again whether the goal I've set is realistic.

I experiment with adjusting the height of my seat and try to find a better angle for my knees. Serious triathletes use different kinds of handlebars so they can stay in a streamlined position for long periods of time. I decide against that.

I stick to the workout program, and am eventually able to bike the full distance, although without the swim and the run as well. My time is still forty minutes over the time allowed, so my only hope is that the entire course will be downhill.

I feel like a real athlete on the bike. I love how my legs produce pure strength, and how the muscles in my arms ripple as I sway back and forth. I might have continued cycling after the event, but it's not enjoyable in my area. After the race, I end up selling my bike.

• • • • •

Running is my favorite, and I'm the least cold doing it. I enjoy the adrenaline rush of hill sprints, which provides an infusion of antidepressants to my brain. I enjoy completing a ten-mile run, and the springy bounce of the treadmill. I like the fact that when I max out the incline and speed, the display reads *Not Recommended.*

As with the other disciplines, I'm not fast. In fact, running makes me cumbersome and awkward. On long road runs, I feel like a bag of rocks being dragged over an uneven surface, heavy and grating. Still, it's easy to measure my progress. Each week I sneak in a few extra miles, and on the rare days that I feel lighter, I am on top of the world.

People usually find the run the hardest part of a triathlon, so that works to my advantage. I know that if I survive the swim and make the bike cutoff time, I should be okay. Three hours is generous. I could practically crawl my way across the finish line, and if necessary, I will.

I learn to love the "bricks," which is the term for a long bike ride followed by a long run. The idea is to get the muscles used to transitioning effectively into running after having exhausted them on the bike. My first few bricks are painful; my legs are useless lumps of clay. But after a lot of practice, my body figures it out, and adjusts itself for maximum efficiency. My success gives me an incredible feeling of power. I reach the end of one discipline and plow right into the next, as if I could keep going forever and ever. I outlast the pain and fatigue. I endure.

I can't say I don't thrive on the physical pain. I'm not the first athlete to say so. However, for me, exercise is not like self-injury. Yes, in part, the stress I put on my body is a way to overshadow emotion, but the goal is different. When I cut myself, it's only about changing the way I feel. With my training, it's about the sense of accomplishment derived from achieving a goal. This gives me boundaries. I can't push myself until I break. I have to eat and sleep and know when to stop. I have to take care of myself.

However, despite the benefits of the program, following it is a little bit like smashing myself into a wall over and over again. The way I feel after a session hardly changes from day to day, and it's disheartening to work so hard and make so little progress. My times are far from those I will need to compete, and I see no way of putting all three sports together without crashing. I'm not sure what would be worse: quitting, or trying and failing. The point is to develop supernatural strength, so I will never feel weak again.

• • • • •

At a horse show, Michele introduces me to a fellow triathlete. Not only has he finished several full Ironmans, he is well regarded at a national level. In addition, he owns some of the biggest and most lucrative horse show venues in the country. To set a good example for his employees, and to show that he is not entitled, he can often be found washing dishes in the cafeteria or cleaning up the grounds. He takes everyone seriously, and is always addressing and fielding the many complaints that come to someone in his position. He is the master of two universes, the epitome of strength and success. I am intimidated, but I can't pass up the opportunity to speak to him.

We sit on the bleachers outside one of the show rings, and I tentatively lay out my training program and explain that I am too slow.

He knows what's wrong right away. "You're overtraining. You lack speed because your training focuses too heavily on distance and too little on intensity. You need to push yourself much harder at shorter intervals instead of going at the same pace for hours. Hill work on the bike, sprints while running, sets for the swim. This will help you go faster overall at the longer distances."

It seems odd to practice for an endurance race by working on short and fast distances, but he is the master. He sits quietly, one long rope of muscle and nothing to prove. I tell him I am a weak swimmer.

"Focus on your arms during the swim. It's the only part of the race in which you really use them, so you can kill them. It's the one part of your body you don't need to conserve. Use your legs to keep you afloat, but don't over work them. You'll need them later. That way you can gain a little speed during the swim without compromising the bike and the run."

This is great advice, and not something I've read about or considered. I move on to a more ridiculous, but important, question.

"Will the lake be cold? I sort of have a problem with cold." *Wow, now I sound really serious*, I think sarcastically.

His response doesn't seem derisive. "Not at all. It's small, and very shallow. In fact, sometimes the organizers ban wetsuits due to the risk of competitors overheating."

I'm endlessly relieved. So much time worrying that hypothermia will cause disorientation on the bike for nothing.

Encouraged, I go on: "And the bike course? Is it flat?"

"Actually, no. It's one of the tougher courses. It's at the base of the Catskill Mountains. Pretty much all hills, both steep and gradual."

My heart sinks. "I'll never finish it in time."

"Practice hills, constantly."

"I do. There isn't really a choice, where I live."

"Then you should be fine." I can't tell if he is trying to keep me positive or if he really means what he says, but I get the impression he is not a man who succeeds on the basis of false hope.

"The hardest part for most people is the transition from cycling to running," he goes on. "It's difficult to switch muscle groups so suddenly, and most people feel pretty wobbly after cycling that far. It's a matter of practice. Spend a lot of time running right off the bike. The first mile will be hell, but push through and it will get easier."

"I've been doing bricks. To be honest, I like the run the most."

"That's going to work to your advantage. Most find that challenging, especially after already having used up so much energy.

"The other crucial aspect is fueling. You'll need to find an energy bar you like, and a pure form of protein you can eat on the bike. For the run, experiment with gels, small amounts of caffeine, and sugar. A lot of this will be provided at aid stations. Then there are the supplements: energy pills, sodium pills, ibuprofen, electrolyte additives for your water. These can be expensive, but they're crucial. Supplements aren't just something that will help; they can make or break your race. You're asking your body to do something unnatural, and you must take its needs seriously. Most triathletes have phenomenal mental strength, so once they realize their body is crashing, it may be too late."

Mental strength.

I thank him profusely and rush off to the show tent to catch up on work. I am overwhelmed, but euphoric. Not only has one of the most successful men in the industry taken me seriously, I have received fantastic advice.

When I arrive at work the next morning, I find he has left me a huge bag of every type of supplement and gel and powder available—hundreds of dollars' worth of the best stuff. I want to cry, and I know that I can't—absolutely can't—fail.

Later, during the show, I fall off a horse. It happens to everyone, and I am thrilled nothing is broken, even though I'm dizzy, everything hurts, and my left arm has a limited range of motion.

Everyone makes me promise to skip today's workout. I agree—but once they have left for the day, I put on my running shoes and do the ten miles mixed with sprints I had planned on doing. I've never felt better. I can do anything.

Ten days before the big day, I begin to taper, drastically cutting down the amount of exercise I do—which is when my knee decides it's had enough. I can hardly walk. I'll compete one-legged if necessary, but this is not good.

"Has it occurred to you that your injury might be psychological? Anxiety-induced?" my dad suggests. That seems silly.

The next day, I am miraculously better. My brain is evil.

I take my bike to be serviced. The servicing costs almost as much as the bike, but so many people don't finish these races on account of mechanical problems, I feel the expense is justified. I pack and repack my carful of equipment, checking everything over and over. There is nothing left to do.

I arrive a day early and go to all the prerace meetings, the ones the pros skip. I ask stupid beginners' questions. I make sure I understand the route and the transitions.

The morning of, I force-feed myself the required breakfast and leave the hotel ridiculously early. Once I arrive at the lake where the race will begin, I sit in the car for a while, not believing this is really it. I have tons of texts on my phone wishing me luck. Leslie offered to come. Actually, a few people did, but this is something I must do alone. I have trained mostly by myself; I have put in so many miles on the road and underwater. At the end of the day, this is about me and my own strength.

I have serious doubts as to whether I will succeed. At no point during practice does the program call for completing the equivalent of the entire event—the recovery time would be too disruptive. So I have no idea if I can do it. There's so much that can go wrong, not all of which is within my control. I don't think I will have it in me to train for the next event if I fail. I feel defeated by the slew of positive messages I receive. The people who support me don't understand that hoping and wanting may not be enough.

The text that finally gets me out of the car is from Lena.

I'm not going to say good luck or assume it's going to go amazing. I support you no matter what happens, and if you don't make it, you're my hero for trying.

It's cool but pleasant in the shallow light of dawn. It's going to be cloudy. Dew hangs softly from the grass, mirroring the damp colors of the lake. I pace around the vendors who are setting up their stalls and try not to feel hugely out of place among the husband-and-wife teams expertly unclipping their bikes from their car racks.

The lake is indeed small, making the swim look shorter than it actually is. I find the spot I've been assigned to transition to the bike and discover it's quite advantageous—right on the edge, and close to the entrance and exit of the transition area. I wonder if my triathlete friend from the horse show had a hand in that. For the hundredth time, I make sure my towel, shoes, and socks are laid out, my pills are tucked into my small bike bag, and my energy bars and cheese sticks are ready to be shoved into my pockets. I put on my wetsuit over my triathlon suit, perhaps for the final time.

Then I'm standing barefoot on the cold, squishy bank of the lake, shaking internally, seeing months and months of training fusing into place. Around me, my fellow competitors are equally excited, but we try to stay still to conserve energy.

When the whistle blows, I force myself to hang back. I'd rather lose thirty seconds than get caught up with the strong swimmers as they thrash forward. A few others do the same, and we smile at each other in comprehension.

Then I'm in the water, splashing through the swishy sediment until I can push off and start the first awkward strokes of the front crawl. The lake is surprisingly warm. I can see the bottom. *This is really it*, I tell myself. The surge of adrenaline is so extreme, I nearly stop swimming. *Get out of your head*, I order myself.

I make myself stay calm and swim slowly, so as not to expend too much energy in the excitement of the moment. As I settle into a slow but consistent rhythm, I can see that I'm far behind the pack; but my split at the halfway mark is just under the cutoff time. When I approach the bank, I can't believe the swim is over. It seems as if only a few minutes have passed since the start of the race, but suddenly I'm out of the water, fumbling out of my wetsuit, drying my feet, and swinging my wet self onto the bike. My time wasn't great, but it was good enough to allow me to proceed.

I spend the first few minutes on the bike replacing some of the calories I have just burned. The hills come immediately, steep and discouraging, and everyone else is going so much faster. But over the next hour, very slowly, I start passing other cyclists—just one or two at first, then quite a few, as the hills take their toll on those who started too confidently.

I am thrilled to find I'm pretty strong on the ascents. The cyclists spread out, and I go for long stretches without seeing anyone. As I enter the woods through which the course travels, the trees loom dark and tall. It starts to drizzle, and the sky's light dims. My trisuit is still wet from the swim, and the soft blanket of water cools my hopes of getting properly dry. But I'm not freezing, and I'm going at a decent speed.

Eventually, the winding path through the woods opens into a wide road, a never-ending expanse of gray concrete. I know I will be on this road for at least an hour and a half.

That's when it happens. Very abruptly, a sheet of water falls from the sky. There are no raindrops—just a solid mass of heavy liquid descending all at once. Through eyes squinted against the assault, I can only see the blurriest outlines of the world. I feel as if am cycling underwater. Even the few cars have pulled to the side of the road.

I discover that it's easier to ride with my sunglasses on, because even though it's night-dark, at least I can keep my eyes open under them. I pass one cyclist, but I'm pretty sure it's a homeless guy, not a competitor.

I am alone for a very long time in the vortex of churning water. When I pass some storefronts, I slow down and see a group of cyclists huddled under an overhang.

"We're gonna wait it out, man," one of them yells at me over the rushing water.

"Oh, heck," another says. "This isn't worth it. I'm going inside to call my wife and have her bring the car."

It feels reckless to continue, but I have no choice. I'm not fast enough to be able to afford a break. I take a breath and force myself onward into the deluge.

Once the surprise of my predicament wears off, I find myself getting very, very cold. I am afraid. I knew the cold would be my downfall; I just expected it to happen in the lake. A ferocious anger takes over my mind, but I know my body will only tolerate so much, and I won't even realize I'm failing until I collapse or veer off the road in confusion.

The only chance I have at avoiding hypothermia is in exceeding my ideal speed in order to generate more body heat. I know I'm risking burnout, but it's the lesser of two evils. I finally come upon several downhill stretches, in contrast to the steep hills at the beginning of the course, but in the driving wind and rain, these stretches are somehow more painful than the ascents. I desperately want to slow down, but I know I can't.

I pass more cyclists who have called it a day in the face of the rain, and finally get to an aid station, where a race official confirms that the race is still underway despite the conditions. He hands me a bottle of electrolyte water that tastes like poison. I drink it.

The gods finally call a ceasefire, and the deluge eases to normal rain. I reach a fork in the road, but the laminated plaque that is meant to indicate the correct route has been washed off the tree on which it was hung, and its arrow is pointing up into the sky.

I stop and deliberate. Two women pull up behind me and start laughing at our predicament.

"If there was ever a sign, this is it. It isn't meant to be today."

Despair rises in me. Months of sweat and blood and early mornings and cold water, and the success of the venture comes down to a washed-out sign?

A van drives slowly by, and a man in the passenger seat rolls down his window and yells, "Go right!" then immediately closes the window as they accelerate away. But who are they? Race officials? Locals joking around?

Their instructions will have to be enough. I leave the ladies behind at the fork and pedal on.

I'm back in the woods. The rain continues to ease up, but I

am extremely cold. I'm already pretty disoriented, but that could be due to the road sign, rather than impending hypothermia. In an attempt to assess my mental state, I do equations in my head. I think I get the calculations right, but I have no way of knowing, and I am not good at math. I am alone on a bike in the middle of nowhere, possibly delirious, and I have a very bad feeling about my situation. I'm still going way too fast, but I don't feel tired—only horribly cold.

Suddenly an aid station appears, and the volunteers in it are cheering, saying I only have a few miles left before the transition to the run. I can't believe it.

As I finally roll the bike into my designated spot, I allow myself some hope. Because of my frantic and reckless speed, I am well within the time allowed, thereby earning myself even more time for the run. I am still soaked through and numb, but running will help.

I permit myself a very short stop to use the bathroom, even though the more serious competitors save time by literally peeing on the bike.

Many have pulled out of the race, but more than half are continuing. We are lunatics, after all.

The run is easy: 13.2 miles along a dirt path. Because of the heavy rain, the ground is saturated and springy. My wet shoes and socks should feel heavy, but my legs work like they have a motor, plowing through puddles while mud splashes into my eyes and mouth.

Even though the run takes several hours, I am energized, and the time passes quickly. The experience is nothing like it was during training. About halfway through the run, it dawns on me that I'm going to make it. I allow myself to run fast, faster than

I have ever gone during practice. It's dangerous, but I am close enough to the end to be able to afford it. I am a perfectly oiled machine calibrated to achieve its full potential. I have never felt like this before.

I glide though the finish strong and exhilarated, in under seven hours. I'm happy, of course—thrilled and proud and relieved. I'm not even tired, and while this is in part due to adrenaline, it is also because I prepared well. In hindsight, I overtrained, but I'm not one to leave anything up to chance.

I gather my soaked and muddy belongings and toss them into the car. I snap a selfie and start spreading the news of my success. I smell of salt and sweat and stale water. I am sticky with dirt, my teal-and-gray trisuit stretched sleekly over my lean form. I will need days to regain the calories I have spent and restore the insult I have done to my body. It might be exaggerating to say I've done the impossible, but it certainly feels that way. I am officially an Ironman. Nothing will ever hurt me again, because I am that strong.

To me, success is sweet only by virtue of having avoided failure. That is valuable, but it's also a little anticlimactic.

I wind my way through the parking lot of cars and bikes and kids, and two hours later, I'm home. Later that evening, as I'm lying on the bed with my bunnies, I receive an email from the race committee.

"Congratulations! We missed you at the awards ceremony. We will mail you your award for a first-place finish in your age group."

It's a kind gesture, but the award doesn't make much of a difference to me. In my mind, this race was never about competing against others—only myself.

• • • • •

I have succeeded. I also realize I have failed. I am the same person I was before I completed the Ironman. If anything, I am more depressed, and feel even more psychological pain. They say this is a common response to achieving a major goal. They say it's because my brain got used to the constant flood of endorphins from exercise, and now it can't regulate itself without them. They say this state will be temporary.

I say, *Maybe I simply didn't try hard enough.*

5. The Attempts

I don't learn from my experience with the Ironman, but I also don't give up. Perhaps my endurance is not the problem. Perhaps it is my strength.

I decide to become a competitive weightlifter. Almost immediately, I am back in my comfort zone: research, training schedules, competition dates—remedies that distract from and overcome the inertia that claws at my receding heels.

The best part of this plan is that it includes Leslie. She owned a gym in a previous life, so she's quite familiar with the specifics of my new quest. She visits the gym recreationally before work, and we coordinate our visits so that I can be in her company. It's wonderful, after the isolation of triathlon training.

I enjoy being with Leslie in the gym setting. It's as if I am being allowed to view another dimension of who she is. In the gym, she is confident and focused, blending in instead of standing out like she does at the barn. Perhaps someone with a sense of self made of steel can afford to be liquid.

The weight-lifting competition consists of three lifts: the

bench press, the squat, and the deadlift. The deadlift involves simply picking up a weight and lifting it from the ground to the hips. The bench press is done lying down, bent arms pushing the bar upward until they are straight. The squat seems highly illogical. For this move, a weightlifter grips the bar behind the neck, lowers themself into a crouch, and then stands again. Technique is essential to safety.

In competition, each movement is performed only once. Those who succeed move on, increasing the weight on the bar and lifting until only the winner remains. When I look up the average amount lifted by women in my body weight category, I am confused. Multiple times my body weight? I'm not an ant, and I have no interest in being crushed into the ground. This is the perfect endeavor.

I love it. I love strutting around the gym in front of the mirrors and pretending to toss heavy plates onto the bar as if they weigh nothing. I love resting on the machines in between sets, watching others go through their workouts, alone, serious, the only sounds their breathing and the sharp clink of metal. I love the physical transformation in my arms and shoulders. I love that each session lasts only forty-five minutes, and that most of that time is spent recovering between lifts. I'm used to five-hour workouts with no breaks. Now it seems I am cheating the system, gaining so much from so little input.

I am not naturally strong. Prolonged periods of exercise are much easier for me than intense single efforts. But if I can succeed in improving my strength as well as my endurance, I will be invincible. Each time I complete a lift, I visualize myself bearing the weight of depression.

Unfortunately, I'm not able to bear that much. The pain is

still there, more so than it has been before. Often, I come to the gym foggy and stand motionless in front of the machines, staring into nothingness.

"Come on," Leslie encourages as she sets the weights for our warm-up routine.

"I can't." Of course, I can, but I want her to say it.

Even though I find it hard to get started, the moment I start pushing or pulling at the weights, nothing exists but the surge of complete mental and physical effort. In that moment, there is no space inside me for the pain. The second I put the weight down, however, the pain comes rushing back with the slowing of my breathing.

Unlike a triathlon, a weight-lifting competition requires that I have a coach. Luckily, Michele, who knows everyone in the universe, sets me up with a friend of hers who just so happens to be one of the most well-regarded and successful coaches in the state. He doesn't take beginners, but Michele pulls strings. I'm determined to show him that he will not regret the favor. I will be the best and most intensely focused beginner ever.

Our first session does not go well. He asks me to show him what I've been doing, and I try adding just a little more weight than I'm used to and utterly fail to lift it on my first few tries. I'm further embarrassed when he very kindly says, "That's good, that's good—but a little much for you right now. You're not quite ready for that. We're going to spend a few months on your technique, without adding any weight, and then start with dumbbells."

Oh, boy.

I like that he is humble and unassuming, wearing loose clothing so as not to show off his godlike physique. I like that he is African American and soft-spoken, and that he doesn't touch me, professionally or otherwise.

I find myself becoming increasingly depressed—but luckily this activity isn't particularly hard to engage in. I can spend many minutes sprawled out on the mats, ostensibly gathering my physical strength for the next lift.

When horse show season comes around, I drag some weights up from my landlord's basement and set them up in my room.

I don't especially want to compete in weightlifting the way I wanted to in the triathlon. It's just that I need the goal, the measurements to stay motivated. It's the only way I can operate. I doubted myself unnecessarily last year, but it really doesn't seem as if I am strong in single bursts of effort at all. My body type is far more suited to endurance sports than power lifting. I tell myself it doesn't matter. If I can succeed on both ends of the spectrum, I will be invincible.

About eight months after I begin my new training regimen, my alarm goes off, letting me know it's time to go to the gym; but I don't get up. I'm not especially depressed—at least, no more than usual. I have a goal, and that's usually a foolproof way of guaranteeing action. But time slips by, and I'm still in bed. The deliciousness of not moving taunts me, and I roll my eyes at the lunacy of the temptation.

It's taking longer than usual for the motivation to kick in, but I don't panic. This happens sometimes. I've never quit anything. The horror of what giving up might mean so drastically outweighs the struggle of continuing that all I need is a quick glance into the abyss of failure before I scurry away from the cliff in shock. Now, however, I peer down into the horror of defeat and expect to be forcefully repelled—and nothing happens. I feel nothing, other than a very hollow sense of wonder. Is it actually possible?

I know that if I give in to this apathy even once, it will be the end. If I slack off, there will be no returning the next day. My game only works in accordance with Newton's first law: *an object in motion . . .*

I quit. I sully everything I have stood for. I violate every principle that keeps me alive. I cave to instant gratification, even while understanding exactly how much I will pay for it in the long run.

I brace myself for the impact of having jumped off the cliff—but the landing is soft and sweet. There's an enormous sense of relief, and guilt—but the relief wins. Somehow, what I've done is a victory in itself.

"Leslie, I quit weightlifting."

"That's fine."

"It's not."

"You're being dramatic. You can come back to it when you're ready—tomorrow, or a year from now. It's not going anywhere."

"I won't come back to it. It's done. I'm done."

"That's fine too!"

"It's not. I'm not me anymore. I gave up the good part of me. Only the bad part is left. You won't like me."

"Don't be ridiculous. It doesn't work that way. Find a new goal. Or don't, and take a break."

But I'm not being ridiculous, and it does work this way. This is not me, and I don't want to know who I am now.

• • • • •

I'm a quitter, and now I'm both mentally and physically weak. So when a new opportunity presents itself, I am intrigued. Perhaps all the exercise was not the cure. Perhaps I need something entirely different. I decide to go to prison.

I hear about it through our vet, one of the few men I trust and am comfortable around. He teaches a life skills course at a maximum-security prison an hour away, and I ask him if he would like a teaching assistant. I have a psychology degree from Vassar, I can spin words into potentially profound statements, and I have an odd affinity for public speaking. I have no life skills whatsoever, but that seems irrelevant. He says yes immediately.

It's perfect—clever and bold. Everyone will think I am altruistic and brave. No one will know my real motive. I have some convoluted and poorly constructed idea that I will feel better if I face my fear: not merely of men, but of men who are actually dangerous. I will forgive them, even help them recover. After all, behind almost every perpetrator lies a victim. This heroic gesture will transcend my earthly problems. Perhaps seeing the prisoners might also serve as a warning: This could also be my destiny, if I don't get my bad behavior under control. Never mind that you go to prison for hurting others, rather than for hurting yourself.

The process of receiving clearance is wildly and thrillingly complicated. They seem concerned that I might be some kind of voyeur with a predilection for criminals. I go to many interviews; I fill out form after form; I gather references. It's funny how hard it is to go to prison if you are innocent. I wait almost eight weeks. When I get my little card granting me access to the other side, I feel as if I have passed a test. I am capable.

Mark, our vet, has been running his life skills program for three years. A day before my first class, he tells me the unofficial rules: Don't reveal a single personal detail. Don't shake hands. Show as little skin as possible; some of these men haven't seen a woman in ten years, aside from the few female guards. Keep redirecting them to the material, and never lose your composure. Remember that there is no real danger; guards will be present at all times.

I pull into the parking lot. It is dark, but apart from the barbed wire fences, the prison could be any type of industrial building. Mark is late, and I hope he doesn't show up, so I can bolt. But he does.

Once inside, I am excessively nervous. Mark assures me it will be easy. I don't find it very easy being stripped of my belongings and passing through the metal detectors. We are allowed paper, but no pens, and no shoelaces or jackets or pockets or hoods. The wide yellow halls are mostly silent as we move through them. The buzzing of the doors, the sharp click as they fall shut, the jangle of keys on the guard's belt are sudden jolts of adrenaline with reverberating echoes. Some of our guards are friendly: we talk about the weather, and they seem to appreciate our efforts. Some are gruff and jaded, perhaps only on the right side of the cage through strokes of luck, and they surely think we are wasting everyone's time. I try to look professional and efficient, as if my life skills are overflowing in their abundance, as if I am not a churning cauldron of fear, my only skill my own idiotic bravery.

When I thought about the prisoners I would be meeting, I imagined deformed old men drooling and slumped over in their chairs, cursing at us as we try to convince them that words are a better form of communication than knives. They are nothing like that. As they file in, I try to assess everything at once. They are mostly young, even attractive. They are not wearing offensive orange, but plain beige over white undershirts. They look like little boys in uniform. Instead of tense hostility, they radiate relaxed amicability. Forgetting the rules immediately, I extend my hand to one in greeting, and stop just short of using my full name. Now I've touched a real-life prisoner—bonus points!

Many of the men thank us immediately for coming, sit down, and eagerly hold their prison-issued miniature pencils poised over journals open to blank pages. This could be easy, after all. Apart from the bare walls and the guards with their guns and various other frightening-looking apparatus, this could be a first-grade classroom, everyone fresh and eager to listen and learn.

Mark lays out the curriculum: the formation of values, mindfulness, personality styles, communication and listening, conflict management, family relations, goal setting, interview tips. The men seem eager to participate, as if this is the first time anyone has truly listened to them, asked their opinion, taken them seriously. One by one, they share their motivations and goals.

"I value my family above all. They are my reason to keep trying. I miss my daughter the most."

"My number one goal is my sobriety. All my mistakes have come from being high."

"When I get angry, I shut down. I don't listen, and I don't communicate."

"I accept that I am here, and trust God to help me along a better path."

"I know that I am an extrovert, so I need to be around people to gather strength."

"I want to work on being more respectful—not only to those around me, but also toward myself."

"I just need to get out of here."

"I'm in for life. I have to make the best of it."

"I like it here. It's easy. Free food. A place to sleep."

Ethan, who is around my age, claims his only crime is living in the state of Connecticut, where marijuana isn't legal. He looks me in the eye and makes comments so intelligent I am unable to recreate them. It's a joke, me teaching him. He knows this, yet throughout the course he is always polite, genuinely thanking me for coming each week. When we conduct mock job interviews, I'd certainly hire him over myself. If he weren't incarcerated.

"It's not at all what I expected!" I say with wonder while stacking chairs at the end of the first class. Sheets of tension are falling off me in layers. "I mean, they're more friendly and respectful than some men on the outside."

Mark nods. "Yeah, they're good guys. This is a hand-picked group. They have to express an active interest in attending, and the warden selects cases that are most likely to succeed, either after release or within the prison community. They're mostly here on drug convictions, or were peripherally involved in an incident."

So much for generously facing, forgiving, and rehabilitating those who have committed heinous crimes.

In fact, I identify with addicts. Even though I have never experimented with illegal drugs, I am also addicted, to the calm and safety I feel in Leslie's presence. If I thought a pill or an injection could get me to the same mental space her presence brings me, I wouldn't hesitate to take it. Who am I to stand before this group, pretending I got life right and they didn't? The line between good and bad isn't just a prison door.

Still, the work is worthwhile. I incorporate dialectical behavior therapy, the same system I used for myself in North Carolina, into the curriculum. Perhaps the prisoners will be able to apply its strategies for emotional and conceptual regulation better than I could. I put the degree my parents paid for to use, referencing relevant psychological research. We watch *Freedom Writers* and read poetry. The prisoners' favorite session involves a simplified version of the Myers-Briggs personality indicator. Introspection comes naturally to me, but some of these men are just starting to use it as a tool. They love finding themselves among the descriptions of traits, and are surprised to learn that both Mark and I are extreme introverts.

At the end of the course, we award each prisoner a personalized certificate. As someone accustomed to receiving academic and athletic awards, I wonder whether the laminated paper they have earned for consistently showing up will be meaningful to them. It seems it is. As Mark points out, this is the first time many of them have been recognized in a positive capacity. I remember the unbridled excitement of receiving my first ribbon as a kid, how I held onto that little prize and how it made me want to try harder. How much of success is simply dependent on positive reinforcement?

The local newspaper writes an article about our class, and Mark asks me if I am up for a second year. But the evening drive to the prison is long and dark, and I have not fooled myself: teaching life skills is not the same as owning them. I have not managed to decrease my own pain by trying to help decrease it in others. I'm too selfish for that.

I decline to continue assisting with the program. In the end, Mark withdraws as well, opting not to teach any additional years.

• • • • •

I am tired and angry and frustrated. If happiness is a matter of determination and hard work, I surely ought to stand before an avalanche of well-being. Instead, I am an animal trapped in a cage. I want to act out, be bad; but I don't know how. I want to be reckless and destructive—cause mayhem and chaos, drama and excitement. Yet my need for control is too strong, my desire to be well-behaved too prominent. But if I don't find a way to decrease the volume of pain, or at least communicate it in a way that will be heard, it will inevitably overflow.

Sometimes I forget that there is life outside my head, that others have far greater problems and would perhaps do anything to be as fortunate as I am. For example, Leslie's mother dies.

It is not unexpected—perhaps even a blessing of sorts—but that doesn't minimize the shock and sadness, the sense of loss and devastation. Leslie and her mother had always been close; her father already deceased.

Finally, my chance has come to be supportive of Leslie, as opposed to the other way around. I will rise to the occasion. It is the perfect opportunity to step outside my own suffering and acknowledge someone else's; to give back a fraction of what I get. It's not about acting out; it is a type of acting in. For Leslie, I can increase the capacity of my cup instead of decreasing the volume of its poison. Opportunity always seems to find me.

Initially, I am quite successful. Leslie is three hours away in Boston for the funeral, and for the first three nights I send her short, appropriate emails with pictures of her favorite horses, reassurances that everything is well at home and I am thinking of her. There is not a single mention of my problems. This is not about me. Leslie seems appreciative, and while I am suffering without her, for once it is for a worthwhile and noble cause.

But my internal panic escalates, and I am having a hard time keeping it in check. The thought of Leslie herself in crisis only adds to my own. Leslie is, by definition, always strong, always okay, always capable of handling me, and herself, in any situation. It cannot be otherwise, or the already tenuous structure of my life will collapse. I don't even know when she is returning.

Surprisingly, there is a part of me that is not entirely selfish. I genuinely love and care about Leslie, and the thought of her being unhappy generates true empathy. I am at least grateful to realize I'm still capable of that.

On Saturday morning, I move about the barn in a trance. I am disoriented by my emotions, which are spinning in all directions. Inevitably, they splash out of control, and I hurry behind the barn and start crying. The leaves are soggy and cold underfoot. Everything about this world is lifeless and raw. I can't go on—I don't know how, and I don't want to.

There is only one way out. I must call Leslie.

The sense of defeat is crushing. I can't even step outside of myself for a few days in order to offer support, or at very least not add to her problems. The pain wins; it always gets its way. With shaking hands, I dial Leslie's number, torment and relief fighting so violently I can barely breathe.

"Hi," she answers cheerfully.

"Hi," I try, not sure what I sound like.

"What's going on?"

"I'm . . . I'm sorry to call. I didn't want to bother you. I just . . ."

"It's no problem; you can always call me."

"How are you?" I attempt, in a pathetic effort to be a reasonable human being.

"I'm hanging in. You?"

How can I say that I'm not, given our circumstances? I hate myself.

"I miss you. I'm not doing so well without you." My voice betrays my efforts not to sob, but dropping the pretense that I'm fine is too tempting.

"Don't worry, you're going to be okay," she says gently. "I'll be back very soon." Regardless of circumstance, we fall into our natural roles.

"I'm going to try to work now," I say, slightly encouraged.

"Sounds good. Talk soon!"

Guilt is shoved behind the relief of instant gratification. I go about my day, still fragile, but at least capable of doing some of my work. As the afternoon drags on, I find myself sinking back into despair; but the funeral is this afternoon. Even I won't call Leslie during the funeral.

Lena arrives to ride, and everyone instantly flocks around her, offering condolences, asking if she needs anything. Not only has her grandmother passed away, but without Leslie, she is more lost than I am. Still, her access to Leslie is unlimited, and being the boss's daughter, she has an army of friends and employees at her disposal. They make plans to take her to dinner and spend the evening with her, to ensure she is not alone and upset.

I'm not quite self-centered enough to believe that the death of a loved one is on the same plane as my childish jealously and turbulent depression, but that doesn't mean my suffering isn't real. I've been working relentlessly at finding a way to reduce the pain, without success. Now Leslie is in crisis, and the crack I perceive in her omnipotence is destabilizing. Not only is she both physically and emotionally less accessible to me than usual, but I also see one hundred percent of the support I crave being directed elsewhere—toward Lena. My anguish is too great to contain, but conveying it at this particular time will come across as resentment that I am not the center of attention. I don't think I can find a way to express my exhaustion and desperation accurately, and I can't take the chance that I will be discredited or dismissed.

I arrive home and find myself in uncharted territory, an odd calm enveloping the screeching pain. This is because I know some form of action must take place. It's not possible for me to remain in this excruciating state. This state of numbness allows me to formulate a plan.

In the moment, I don't fully understand what I'm trying to achieve; but in hindsight it is quite clear. Within me are bottomless unmet needs, and I must find a way to have them met.

All my life, I've cut as a way to reduce the internal pain; but this time is going to be different. This time I will cut to damage, so much so that I will need medical attention. I will force someone to help me.

I gather fresh razors and towels and lay them out on the bathroom counter. My heart is hammering so hard that I feel the pulse in my eyeballs. Sweat and adrenaline seep out of me—a horrible feeling, but vastly preferable to everything else.

As usual, I need to focus hard to make the first incision. I have no intention of dying, because no one can help me if I'm dead. But if my cut is too shallow, I will be laughed at for seeking medical attention, and I can't risk that.

As usual, I allow myself to warm up: a few small cuts to set the stage, test the blade's sharpness, assess my willingness to press down. I choose the back of my arm because I don't want to risk cutting too close to a vein. I'm ready.

The first cut is not deep enough. Neither is the second. It's surprisingly difficult to override the instinct for self-preservation. A surge of hot anger and bitter frustration rushes through me.

I take a moment and summon everything I feel—desperation. Unfairness. Abandonment. Disappointment. Loneliness. Torment. And in the moment when these feelings eclipse anything and everything else, I sink the blade.

At first, it doesn't hurt. The skin parts, and there is no blood—only the mottled whiteness of my insides. Is this the problem? Am I empty on the inside?

Then the blood flows, a wonderful, overpowering flood inside my head, like a dam has broken. Endorphins rush in so fast and far that I feel nothing else, and it's blissful. I quickly make use of this state and make more cuts, just in case one is not enough to be taken seriously.

I'm done. The success of having made the cuts and decreased the pain is intoxicating. There is blood on the counter and on the floor, and decapitated razors are strewn everywhere. In a move that is very much unlike me, I leave the mess, grab a new towel, and head out the door. I deserve this.

On the drive to the ER, I start having doubts. Did I do enough to warrant help? Am I going to be laughed at—treated as a sad young adult with nothing better to do on a Saturday night? I keep checking my arm to make sure it's still bleeding.

Hesitant and afraid, I arrive at the hospital and take a seat in the waiting room. It's quite empty; there's a man reading a newspaper, and a middle-aged woman pacing about looking bored. An old lady is slumped in a chair close to the entrance. She tries to smile at me, but instead grimaces in pain. I stay close to the door as well, because I'm not sure I'm supposed to be here.

An intake nurse comes over, not friendly, not unfriendly, and asks which of us was here first.

I don't speak, so the elderly lady does. "I was, honey." Her voice is shaky and slow. "But this girl here should be seen first. Look at her arm."

The nurse looks over and nods. I am mortified. I don't even have a real injury, and I'm not about to bump this sweet woman who is in obvious pain out of her place in line. She can't help whatever happened to her. I could have.

"Absolutely not. I'm fine," I say vehemently. "It doesn't even hurt." It's the truth, and I wave my arm, still wrapped in a towel, in demonstration.

The nurse nods again and turns back to the woman, asking her what happened.

"I fell and hurt my neck," she whispers meekly. To me, she says, "Honey, you are just too kind."

I feel like the world's biggest fraud. Once she has been taken away in a wheelchair, the nurse asks me to unwrap my arm. I do.

"How did this happen?" she asks. Not kindly, not unkindly.

I haven't thought this far. "I was opening a box. With a box cutter. And I slipped." Five times. On the back of my arm.

She nods and motions me to follow her further into the ER. I exhale. I am being taken seriously enough to have been invited inside.

The corridor is empty and quiet. It seems as if most people

do indeed have better things to do on a Saturday night. I am told to sit on an inclined table in a little cubicle filled with medical equipment.

I wait for a while, but I don't mind, taking in the clean, bright space, reading the signs and charts, allowing myself to feast my eyes on the array of monitors, probes, jars of sterile equipment. I think of Lena at dinner with our coworkers and friends, and it doesn't hurt anymore. What I have now is better.

A new nurse comes in, young and smiling and cheerful, and asks me what happened. I'm done lying. "I said it was a box cutter that slipped, but actually, I did it myself, with a razor blade." The words come out quickly, sufficiently tinged with embarrassment and contrition.

"Don't worry. We're here to help you, not judge you," she says kindly, and I am momentarily shocked into silence.

The doctor arrives and asks what happened to me. Don't these people communicate? When I answer, he sighs and doesn't say anything. I know he thinks I am a waste of his time, and I am, but I don't care. He took an oath. He has to fix my injury, whether he wants to or not.

I watch his work with fascination and pleasure. This is what I sought—attention, others to help me when I could no longer do so myself. He works slowly, thoroughly, and carefully. When he injects anesthetic and asks whether I can feel anything, I say no. It's the most wonderful question—and the most wonderful answer.

The work takes a while, and there are so many stitches. Even the warm-up cut gets some, which pleases me endlessly. I am worthy. After he finishes, my whole arm is carefully wrapped in a clean white bandage, and I feel considerably better.

As the doctor turns to leave, he informs me I will be staying in the ER overnight for my own safety. I tell him this isn't necessary; I am fine now and have no intention of harming myself further. Also, I have to feed my bunnies and be at work early the next morning.

But apparently, it's nonnegotiable. I begin to think that I am perhaps not that clever after all. If I miss work, Leslie will find out what I've done, and this cannot happen. She just buried her mother, and I will not add to her stress. This was never meant to go public.

I begin to worry, and call one of my coworkers. I tell her I am in the ER, and she is sensitive enough not to inquire further. She promises to cover my hours until I can get to work and insists she will not say anything to anyone. She keeps her word.

I call my landlady, who lives in the same building as me. She agrees to feed the bunnies, and I know I can trust her. This isn't exactly the outcome I had intended, but it will have to be good enough.

I am too wired to sleep, so I close my eyes and rest, which the reduction in pain has at least made possible.

Close to midnight, my phone rings. This can't be good. No one ever calls me at this hour. Perhaps something is wrong with the bunnies, or my coworker has changed her mind about covering for me. But when I look at the display and see who's calling, my heart explodes in confusion and fear. It's Leslie.

"Hello?" I say, very tentatively.

"Where are you, baby?" I can't read anything in her voice, but hearing it is better than any anesthetic.

"I . . . why do you ask?" I'm still hoping she doesn't know

what has happened. It really wasn't a trick to get her attention—
not at a time like this.

"El, your landlady called me."

I can't figure out why.

"Because when she went to feed the bunnies, she found what
looked like a crime scene in your bathroom. She was worried
and disturbed. I had to explain to her what self-injury is." She
doesn't sound angry, only tired.

I'd completely forgotten I left a mess, because I never do. I
burst into tears. Leslie knows the truth.

"I didn't want you to know! I wasn't going to tell you, I
swear! It's not fair to you. No one was ever supposed to find out.
I wasn't going to involve you when you have so much else going
on. I didn't want you to know. Please believe me. I'm sorry; I'm
so sorry." All the emotion of the past twelve hours overflows into
a river of hysterics, and I can't form any more words.

"El, don't worry." Now she sounds the way she always sounds,
calm and friendly and understanding. "Why don't you tell me
what happened, from the beginning."

I tell her about the intolerable pain, about not wanting or
being able to call during the funeral, about the absurdity of feeling so awful in light of her own situation. I tell her how seeing
everyone interact around Lena pushed me over some invisible
edge, and that I had to do something in order to stay alive.

"You did what you felt you had to do. I know you weren't
trying to hurt me. Yes, it came at a bad time, and I'm not always
going to be able to pick up the phone when you call. But that
doesn't mean I'm not always here for you. I'm going through
a lot right now, but that doesn't mean you aren't, too. I'm not
angry; I understand. I understand that the position Lena is in is

a difficult one for you. It can be a difficult one for her as well. But everything's fine."

All I can do is cry, because I love Leslie and she understands me, and with that knowledge, I can deal with the pain.

"Do you want me to come see you? I'm a couple hours away, and I'd have to go back in the morning, but if you want, I'll come."

I am overwhelmed by the magnitude of her strength and generosity. The least I can do is say no, which I am able to do, because knowing she would come if I said yes is enough. I am full of shame and relief and wonder.

Leslie does tell me I'm going to need to come clean to Jen about missing work tomorrow morning. I give Jen a weak account of the truth. She isn't happy, but there are no consequences.

After work, I drag myself up to my apartment and find no evidence of the mess I made the night before. I mentally thank my landlady. My head hurts quite a bit, and my arm hurts a little, but both distractions are welcome. The world is washed out in a pale light, and the temperature won't commit to hot or cold. I'm exhausted. How do I end up in these situations?

I know the answer. I can distract myself with various endeavors; but when they are over, nothing is different. I end up in these situations because sometimes, everything I do to stop, ignore, or diffuse the pain fails. Because the energy inside me needs an outlet. Because the need for Leslie always wins. Because despite the sense of failure, when I look at my stitches, a part of me believes I did something right.

6. The Cutting

It was my idea. I didn't know at first, that I wasn't the only one. I didn't see it on TV or read about it in a magazine. I didn't copy a friend, or try it on like a borrowed shirt. It was something I did just for me—mine in its entirety, as much a part of me as my skin and bones.

That first time, it happened because something needed to change. I couldn't say what—only that an event needed to occur to curb the existential restlessness and inexplicable unease building inside me.

It was an evening like any other. I was about to climb into bed, but first I unbent a paper clip and scratched a short line onto the back of my hand. It was truly a nonevent—like switching out a light. It seemed like the right thing to do, a natural act. I had created a little change, made by me and for me. I looked at the little pink line, and looked forward to seeing it scabbed over by morning.

Soon, I graduated from a paper clip to a razor. The first time I did more than scratch the surface of my skin, I was horrified and thrilled. I had discovered the power to transform the pain—not in magnitude, but in deliberation and intent. It was a skill that, once discovered, I guarded and treasured.

Before long, that transformative power blossomed into its real function: I found that I could take the emotional pain and redefine it as physical pain, using self-inflicted cuts as a means of turning undesirable emotions into a clean, honest, comprehensible problem. Each line was an expression of that which demanded existence in the tangible realm. It is so much easier to understand the concrete.

Every time emotional discomfort of any magnitude confronts me, I cut. In my mind I summon the greatest concentration of distress capable of fitting into a few seconds, and in that window, I draw the cut.

I still find the same release in the act, all these years later. For that brief moment when I draw the blade over my arm, the sharp sting of parting skin is greater than everything else; it overrides, kills, erases whatever emotion I have laid out in surrender. One pain is exchanged for another; but the latter is devoid of content—clean, pure, explainable, and controllable.

Anything that matters must surely leave a mark—a history, a change, an acknowledgment of itself, a voice crying that something happened, it exists, it is real. Each cut is a visual reminder that the invisible pain is there—direct damage dealt by an unquiet mind. I need this manifestation to know that I have not imagined the internal chaos. Each scar is a validation. It says, *Yes, it was so; you are not crazy.*

The process is the same every time. I gather the painful thoughts and allow them to run in a perfect parallel to the cut. I am responsible for deciding what internal damage is worthy of a wound. I must balance my own universe.

Cutting keeps me alive by allowing me to choose how I experience pain. I cut so that emotions don't kill me. I can't keep them away forever, but the cut provides a brief distraction, a generous reprieve during which I can tighten my resolve to keep fighting. It's not a punishment for being weak; it's a reward for remaining strong. There is something cathartic, symbolic, about the release; watching the blood flow and the tension drain, the deep red a visceral contrast against the darkness inside. A snapshot of calm to hold onto.

The second it's over, healing begins. I can stitch or bandage or medicate, the way I wish I could do with my mind. I can clean up the mess, rest beneath the gentle pressure of the wrap, allow myself to be lulled by the soft throb that follows the blinding pain.

In the moment, it's the only option in the face of none. Under different circumstances, perhaps there would be other ways, but a person tossed into a stormy sea will reach for a life raft, not work on improving the quality of his stroke. There is a time and place for training, and a time and place for staying alive.

We have a relationship, cutting and I. It's not dysfunctional, abusive, or addicting. Rather, it's nurturing, reliable, and enduring. It's there when I need it; it gives me space when I don't. It's a vessel for that which cannot be contained. We are in love, yet completely separable and independent. I can imagine a future without it—but I don't need to.

To me, cutting has nothing to do with dying and everything to do with fighting to live. It poses little risk to my life, but it does leave scars, a quiet road map to survival. I like the scars; proof of a war I'm willing to fight.

Ritualistically, I am allowed a few warm-up cuts to get a feel for the sharpness of the blade before I go in for the real damage. I cut until I make an incision I'm happy with, though I do not get unlimited tries. Some days, I can't get my hand to press deeply enough, and I taunt myself by concluding that my suffering must not be worthy of a real cut, and the resulting rage is usually enough to compel action.

I need to watch the skin break open, mirroring the way everything feels broken inside. In the second before the blood wells up, I look down into the abyss, trying to find the answer within. There is never enough time, and there is never an answer. Soon the blood wells, calling out that I am still alive.

On some days, cutting doesn't work as effectively. Or, if the emotional pain is too great and the corresponding cut could kill me, I don't allow myself to try. Cutting is reserved for the times the pain reaches the upper ranges, but not a peak. On the other hand, if the emotional pain is not great enough, I don't allow myself to cut, either. I never cut to die, and I never cut for fun.

For me, cutting is safe—rational, controlled, and natural. Cutting is the solution—the problem is everything else.

And then, the problem becomes every*one* else.

Drinking, smoking, drugs, eating disorders, promiscuous sex—all acknowledged as maladaptive but commonplace coping mechanisms, all a form of self-injury, self-destruction— perhaps all indicative of some type of suffering, and sometimes a cause of suffering on their own. Cutting is no different: there is a price, and a reward. Yet I have found that many view it as something else: dangerous, repulsive, incomprehensible. This just never occurred to me.

When I first started cutting, I didn't hide it. It didn't feel wrong or shameful; if anything, it felt intelligent.

My parents noticed the scratches first.

"That's not an intelligent thing to do. You're asking for an infection. And it could leave a scar."

That was all they said. Their words were logical, unemotional—and certainly no deterrent.

I kept cutting. Sometimes I hid it; sometimes I didn't. I received similar admonitions, but I still didn't see the big deal. Sometimes I would tell people about it—relatives or friends. It wasn't a ploy for attention; I didn't consider it interesting. It was just another thing I did, something else I sometimes enjoyed: *I like horses, and I like to cut myself.* When friends copied me, it felt no different than them watching a movie I had told them about.

Thinking back now, I can see so many points at which my trajectory could have run differently. People who might have stopped me, or kept asking why until they hit the bottom. But at the time, I don't believe even I had access to the bottom. I'm not sure I could have found it, even with help. Pain seeks to run its course, the possible variations in its path only practical, not elemental. It's no one's fault. No one should assume pneumonia based on a sore throat, and to medicate as such would be irresponsible. While I was in discomfort, I had no way of knowing, factually, whether it was normal or not. How could I know where on the continuum I fell?

I was naive, and it took me a while to realize that many people opposed my behavior, labeled it *bad.* But that wasn't a problem. I simply began to cut under places covered by clothing.

Then I came to realize something interesting: my rational solutions for undesirable emotions might be indicative of a more serious problem. A few people suggested I might need some form of help. Help would have been fantastic, however effective it proved. Cutting might have been a bridge to get there, the proof required. But until then, I had seen it like a distant mirage, lacking reality or substance.

Did I need therapy? As I understood it, therapy was something you were dragged into because the rest of the world couldn't stand your craziness. I was well-behaved, got good grades, played sports, and had a few good friends. No one wanted to drag me anywhere, and I couldn't possibly suggest they do so. What kind of narcissist thinks their problems are worthy of professional help? And yet, help was what I craved—to be safe, to be *saved*.

During my freshman year of high school, I had a teacher who, though he was boring and unsympathetic, sharply caught my attention in three sentences.

"As teachers, we have a responsibility to look for warning signs. Unexplained injuries, eating disorders, self-inflected harm. By law, we must come forward with any suspicions."

I was worthy of action. Better still, I could use what came naturally to me to attract those who might be able to help. I could give a warning sign. A warning sign of what, I had no idea.

I started cutting the backs of my hands, and added a few burns as an insurance policy in case the cutting wasn't enough. Nothing serious, but too consistent to be ruled accidental. Then I waited.

Nothing happened. Once the injuries faded, I came to a conclusion: my problems were invisible, not serious enough. I was an imposter—or maybe my teacher's little speech had just been for show.

Still, I didn't give up entirely. The following year, I told a different teacher, one whom I surmised might be supportive, about my cutting. I pretended it was a behavior I wanted to stop, and that I would like help doing so. I hated lying, but I couldn't exactly say, "I cut, but it's for me. I have no intention of stopping, but I want someone to listen."

It worked this time. She seemed concerned, and suggested I visit the school counselor. "Try five sessions and see how you feel," she suggested amicably.

I was elated. I felt important, sitting in the counselor's office.

"We wouldn't want this problem to become more serious." I clung to the word *serious* like a dog with a bone.

It was my one shot at salvation.

The office was fairly big, and cluttered with personal items: paintings, books, figurines. The counselor himself was short and overweight. I knew I couldn't afford to dislike him, or to wish he were female. I was actually stupid enough to believe that perhaps mental health was a man's profession.

"What brings you here?" he asked. I didn't like the question. My suffering was supposed to be self-evident. I had expected that as a professional, he would tell *me* what the problem was.

"A teacher."

"Do you want to be here?"

"Yes." I sounded needy.

"And why is that?"

I didn't know what to say. "Because . . . I don't think . . . I'm happy." It was the lamest thing I'd ever said.

At the next session, I filled out a very long questionnaire. Perhaps the results would tell him what was wrong with me.

During our third session, he asked me to fill out the questionnaire again. "We did this last time," I said.

"I lost it. Do it again."

This seemed unprofessional, but I figured maybe a doctor didn't need to follow the same rules as everyone else.

On the fourth session, he brought a boy into the room, perhaps a few years younger than me. We sat on the couch in silence for a very long time. I thought it must be a special kind of experiment. After a while the counselor launched into a long lecture about how we had failed to interact, even though we were both passionate individuals. We were dismissed, and we half-smiled and shrugged at each other on the way out. It wasn't at all what I expected, being saved. It occurred to me that he had probably just double-booked.

During the fifth session, I decided it was time to use my trump card. To my relief, there were no other patients in the room with me, and he seemed not to have lost the second questionnaire.

"I cut myself."

"Where?"

"Pretty much everywhere."

"Can I see?"

I pulled off my sweater; I had a tank top on underneath. I told myself it must be fine, even mandatory, to undress in front of a doctor. The cuts looked weak and small in daylight, but my soul felt exposed.

"That's nothing to worry about. You're a teenage girl. They all do it. It's normal."

And that was that. I had my confirmation in black and white, from the mouth of a doctor: there was nothing wrong with me. My sessions were up, although he said he had room in his schedule to keep seeing me if that's what I wanted. I didn't.

I kept cutting. Sometimes I stopped for long periods of time, but we always came back to each other, like old friends who are so close that distance is immaterial. I played around on the internet and connected with other cutters. It was fascinating, seeing how many others there were.

I decided to try therapy with a female. She wore a very short skirt and told me it was because she would rather have been a professional dancer, but things didn't work out. To the best of my ability, I described what I believed to be wrong.

"The problem is clear to me," she pronounced proudly. "You have bipolar disorder—manic depression. It affects many people your age."

Well, that was simple. I didn't feel bipolar, but it sounded a lot better than plain *pathetic*, so I accepted the label. She started me on Zoloft, and I clearly remember the magical moment when I swallowed my first pill, my happy future. I fell asleep for the next week. While being unconscious was one solution, it was not a practical one, so I stopped taking the medicine.

I told her about the cutting.

"You must stop that. It's an addiction," she said sternly.

I told her I didn't really plan to.

"In that case, I cannot work with you. It's too much of a liability. You'll have to make a choice."

For once, something was easy. I left her office and didn't look back.

Finally, I became sick of myself. It was time to try something more radical.

I arranged to go to a psychiatric hospital for one week. This is what people do. Go to hospitals. Get better. It took a huge amount of effort to convince my parents, but I was adamant.

The facility in our town was supposedly one of the best in

the country. The lawns were neatly manicured. A little bridge rose over a stream on the grounds, and the buildings looked like quaint cottages.

It wasn't at all what I expected. The intake procedure took so long, I wondered if it would take up the entire week. Once I was finally assigned to a house—an unlocked unit—I imagined I would be left alone to rest in my room. I would read and write, and talk to the doctors who would come to fix me.

This was not the case. Instead, I was dragged from group to activity to group. I couldn't see any point to them. Still, I threw myself into the process, determined to allow it to work in ways I couldn't yet fathom. After all, I reasoned, if I could recover on my own, I wouldn't need to be here.

Still, I wasn't sure how smart these people were. I was allowed to shower—and given a razor with which to shave. I could have slashed my wrists, and they'd never have recovered from the lawsuit. I was halfway through a prescription of antibiotics for a self-inflicted burn, but they took the bottle away from me and didn't let me finish the course. Another potential lawsuit.

I could have just walked home. But I didn't.

When the week was over, I expected to view everything through a new lens, clear and bright, without the shadow of depression. But I wasn't sure how I felt.

I was eager to try out my new skills, to test the fixed version of myself. I got out my razor and held it over my skin, expecting it to be physically impossible to move my hand. This was not the case. I was able to make the cut. I was shocked. How was this possible? It was as if I had been to the hospital for an appendectomy, and come home with my appendix still intact.

I was hugely disappointed—but also a little relieved. Cutting was a good friend, and while I was willing to say good-bye, I knew it would not abandon me or let me down.

•••••

Back to the present.

As usual, I am at a horse show. The show is over. The clients fly home. Leslie and Michele depart as well. It has not been a particularly good show, and they are tired and eager to leave. This past month, I have been needier and more desperate than usual, and even Leslie's patience is wearing thin. The pain violently crashes against me like waves onto a cliff, and I'm reeling and disoriented from repeated impacts. There are only so many times Leslie can anchor me within a given day.

I'm beyond reading social cues or taking into account the mental state of others. Leslie has been working around the clock, fielding complaints from clients big and small, dealing with the death of a horse, and worrying over a friend who slipped into a coma following a car accident. My troubles can't compete with hers; but in my frantic state, I believe they can.

Uncharacteristically, Leslie reaches her limit and snaps at me. Michele thinks I'm the most disgraceful, ungrateful being on the planet. My parents don't understand the gravity of my situation. No one does.

I've been abandoned, metaphorically and practically. Leslie and Michele have left. The horses will be shipped home in the morning. I must pack and load them onto the truck before I head to the airport. This is the problem, and also my salvation. Ideally, I'd like to hurt myself quite badly, but there is no one here who can cover for me if I incapacitate myself. However despicable and far gone I might be, I will not abandon our horses so far from home.

In the evening, the pain becomes absurd. It hurts too much to sit still, and it hurts too much to move. I wander around the empty rooms of the rental unit as if in a fun house, everything too large, distorted. I cannot place myself in reality. Perhaps I am hallucinating. I will not be able to survive until morning. I need a plan.

I lie down fully clothed at the bottom of the massive white bathtub and think. I have used up all my coping strategies. I won't even feel it if I cut. It is truly terrifying.

Suddenly, I have an idea. At first it seems rather odd, but thinking about it causes a noticeable decrease in tension, so perhaps I am on to something.

I get out of the tub and remove my clothes. I'm not sure why this is necessary, but it feels right. I am naked, at an elemental level. I move silently into the kitchen, my bare feet sinking into the soft carpet, my body gliding amid the smooth planes of air. I am tiptoeing away from myself, sneaking about before I can be caught carrying out my intent.

The kitchen floor is cool, and my temperature rises in anticipation. I watch my hand reach into the drawer from a distance as I study my selection of knives. Not a sharp one, but a long, dull, serrated one appears in my hand. I hold it and I stare at it, naked and transfixed.

Adrenaline washes over me, and I surrender, knowing I am close to the relief I long for. I feel like an Olympic diver on the board, years of practice backing what will happen in the next three seconds.

I am the diver. The time for practice has come to an end.

This time, there will be no warm-up cut.

I place the blade gently against my cheek and press its little teeth into my skin. I have one chance to make the cut deep enough to be meaningful, but not so deep that it needs stitches—only one chance to win or lose. I am not afraid that I lack resolve, or of the knowledge that I am doing something wholly irreversible. I am willing to sacrifice forever so I can get through this moment. I am ready to cut my face.

I pull back hard on the knife's handle.

I know right away that it's perfect, the way a diver knows in the second he breaks the surface that he has entered the water at the perfect angle and speed, and for a moment I experience the unparalleled feeling of sinking deep into the silent, calming pressure of the pool. When we emerge, the water runs from our shared body, leaving us light and breathing, slightly dazed and in awe of what we have just done.

Calmly, I place the knife in the sink and retrace my steps to the bathroom, where I examine my prize. It's beautiful—a bright diagonal line maybe four inches long, just deep enough, stunningly crimson against white skin. I exhale, shaky and mortified and grateful that I have found a way. I always find a way. I feel safer, less alone; and at least for now, the pain slinks away in defeat.

Unlike a razor, the knife cut wide, but not deep. I clean the cut with soap and water and apply some ointment. Then I throw a towel over the pillow and lie down until it's time to go.

The next morning, I prepare the horses and meet the driver. He does not comment on my appearance. I climb up onto the trailer one last time, double-checking that the horses are comfortable and properly secured. Satisfied that they are, I take a step back, expecting the ramp under my feet. I am the last person to trust my own motives, but I am very sure that what happens next is an accident. There is no ramp—we slid it up a few minutes ago. I step backward into empty space, and when I hit the ground, my knee cracks underneath me.

I know pain—and this is pure, I think I might pass out or throw up. The world is spinning very quickly—a sensation that is, at least, not entirely unpleasant.

The driver rushes over. He helps me to a bench, and I know I must be pretty far gone to let him touch me. After many aggressive assurances that I am fine, and that I will call a friend and see a doctor, he hesitantly returns to the truck, and I wish him a safe journey.

Once he leaves with the trailer, I hop to my car on one leg, fall behind the wheel, and cry. I am destined for destruction.

I struggle back to the house to collect my bags. At the airport, I call Leslie.

"How did the loading go?" she asks.

"The horses were good. I fell off the trailer."

"Are you okay?"

"Yeah. But Leslie?"

"Yes?"

"The thing that happened to my face—it happened when I fell off the trailer, okay?"

"What happened to it?"

"It . . . got cut. When I fell off the trailer."

"Okay."

"I really did fall, accidentally. You have to believe me!"

"I do. The driver called me about it."

"Are you angry? About the face?"

"No. I don't know how to help you, but I wish I did."

That's good enough for me.

I drag myself along the terminal, using my suitcase as a crutch. When I get to my gate, I collapse onto the floor in a pathetic heap. I lean against the wall and prop my throbbing leg onto my bag. Tears wash down my face in a steady torrent, stinging the cut, making it look angrier than it already does. I wonder what people passing by must think of me. I must look like a victim of war, and this is not inaccurate. But no one looks, no one comments. This is an airport, and unless you are a terrorist, anything goes.

When I finally get home, Leslie gives me two days off. I can't tell if this is a reward or a punishment, but I don't care. I spend the entire time lying on the carpet next to Riley, my second bunny—a shy, tiny black creature, the runt of his litter. I sprawl on the floor, staring at him, loving him with all my being. His innocent little presence stares back at me through large brown eyes, and I can feel him loving me, too. He is afraid of being touched, but if I move slowly enough, I can stroke his head with the tip of my finger.

Since Riley refuses to come to work with me the way Jinx did, I bought him a friend so he wouldn't be lonely. Echo turned out to be a small black-and-white monster. At first, Riley seemed cautiously intrigued by him. Then Echo bit Riley's ear, tore up the carpet, gnawed on the walls, and growled when I came near him. My insides cracked when he bullied Riley. I desperately wanted to defend my gentle, loving child; but Echo was mine just as much as Riley was.

Riley, of course, outsmarted us all. He won Echo over. He never challenged the newcomer—just sat quietly until Echo became lonely and fell asleep next to him. They learned to appreciate each other.

Echo turned out to be quite funny, always inventing silly games for himself. One of his favorites is to slide under a towel and zoom around with it covering him, so he looks like a kid playing superhero. Or sometimes he bounces up and down on the sofa, daring me to shoo him off.

Echo is good at making me laugh—but Riley is my soulmate. After my two days are up, my bunnies have filled me with enough love and peace to sustain me for the next few days.

I have a story ready for when I'm questioned about my face, but no one asks. Perhaps they know, or perhaps they don't care. It takes about a year for my knee to heal, and about the same time for the scar to fade to white. It's barely noticeable now, as I'm naturally pale.

I have no plan to stop cutting, and no plan to continue cutting. I'll always be a cutter, active or not. It's who I am.

7. The Summer

After I cut my face, Leslie decides I need to see a new psychiatrist and obtain better medication. Perhaps my behavior is the result of a shifting chemical imbalance. I am willing to try.

I find Jessica online, spend an exorbitant amount of time analyzing her qualifications and patient reviews, and finally make an appointment. She's young and pretty and sharply dressed, which initially makes me nervous. I quickly discover that she is highly motivated and up to date on the current research. She's sympathetic, yet professional. Her fees are astronomical.

In the first session, she takes a detailed history and makes so many notes she looks like a student before an exam. She wants my input, saying this is not a one-sided process. This seems reassuring.

"How come you chose to leave your previous psychiatrist?"

"He was an idiot." I can't read her face, so I elaborate. "I stuck with him for years because he had a prescription pad and I told him what I wanted and he signed it. That worked for a long time. It wasn't too expensive, because I never really saw him.

Every now and then he'd get pompous and tell me it was his duty to check in with me, but he didn't actually know who I was. I'd simply tell him we'd met last month, and he'd believe me. Every time I asked for a refill, I had to introduce myself all over again."

Now Jessica's face betrays a hint of concern and surprise. I'm beginning to enjoy myself, so I go on: "One time I asked to add a new medication to augment my usual antidepressant. I picked it up and spent the next four days and nights wide awake. It was amazing. I felt like I was high. But after a while, I realized something wasn't right, so I did some research and figured out the dosage he had me on was way too strong. Apparently it could have caused seizures if I'd kept it up."

Jessica is clearly horrified. She says she needs to call my old doctor to obtain my records, and I know she'll want to try even if I tell her not to bother. We make minor adjustments to begin with, and I assure her I understand this is a long-term process. These drugs can be very slow to kick in; it may be months before the side effects wear off, and some patients try between five and ten different combinations. I am possibly looking at a year of work. I know what I am in for, and I have no choice.

When I come in for our second session, Jessica looks mortified.

"I had an odd experience last week. As I mentioned, I needed to call your old psychiatrist to obtain your records. When I spoke to him, he seemed to have only a vague recollection of who you were. I asked him for his notes and your medical history, and he became quite rude and offended. He said I was wasting his time, and then he hung up on me." She looks genuinely perplexed and disturbed.

I laugh wryly. "I don't think he keeps records."

She still looks confused. "That sounds unethical. I've never had a conversation like that with another professional."

"I could have told you that. I'm sorry." I feel bad that he was disrespectful, and guilty that I encouraged his lassitude.

Jessica wants to see me every two weeks until we have found a medication and dosage that works for me. She tells me I can and should call or email her in between sessions with any questions or concerns. I plan to do so—properly, this time.

Over the next few months, I feel nothing at best—nauseous, exhausted, or wired at worst. One drug works quite well, but it makes my legs feel like they are on fire. Still, if fiery legs are the price I have to pay for less internal pain, so be it. When I'm moving around the barn, it doesn't even feel that bad. It's when I slow down for the evenings that I start to feel awful. I stick it out, but after a few weeks, the medicine stops working altogether, giving me permission to quit.

Then I hear of something that sounds promising. It's an antidepressant that doubles as a treatment for unexplained nerve pain, also known as fibromyalgia, and has proven useful for those who experience depression in a very physically painful way. I didn't even know there were others like me. This is it—my holy grail.

With Jessica's approval, I take this medication for a week, and then two. I expect to feel better. If nothing else, the placebo effect should help. Eventually it kicks in. Unfortunately, it makes the pain worse, and I become sluggish, foggy and weak.

"I think you need to move on, El," Leslie says.

"How do you know?" I slur.

"I really don't. I just want to be supportive."

I call Jessica. "It's not working."

"Okay. Let's slowly discontinue it and look into other options next session."

"What if it just needs more time to work?"

"That's possible."

"So what should I do?"

"It's your decision. Only you know how you really feel."

Isn't that true. I respect her for understanding this. I toss out one more chance at a future.

• • • • •

We enter the summer show season, touring all around New England. During the rare week that I'm home, I don't bother unpacking. It's a terrible time to be experimenting with my body and mind, but there is no good time.

Working at shows is brutal. Showing takes place Wednesdays through Sundays, with Tuesday as a setup day, and Monday as a rest day if we're lucky. We get up around four a.m., but we aren't tired—we are too anxious about coordinating the hundred things that have to be done before eight a.m. I help with the barn work, and then ride several horses to the rings for a morning school, where they work off nervous energy, get a look at the current setup of the course, and receive a quick refresher on the important commands. The idea is to make them as calm as possible, so that their owners can show them.

From eight to six we deliver the animals to their respective show rings, where they meet trainer and client. It takes a little over an hour to make each horse presentable and to put it away after an event. The work is fast-paced, and mistakes cannot be made. We are afforded little time, if any, to eat or drink. Temperatures often reach a hundred degrees, so the horses have efficient fanning setups and cold-hosing schedules. We don't stop for rain. We get very, very wet, and cleaning the mud off the animals and equipment takes double the time.

We have an hour for dinner before we return to the show in the early evening. We put in a few more hours of work, making sure the horses are happy and comfortable and that everything is ready for tomorrow. When we finally get home, we collaborate with the trainers to plan a schedule for the next day. By that time, we are all so tired, we end up writing each other notes or sending texts at all hours of the night.

There's also my own showing. Some owners prefer to watch their horses perform from the sidelines. In this case, I quickly shed my sweat-or-water drenched outfit and wriggle into perfectly pressed show clothes. An instant transformation. I learn the course and warm up the horse under Leslie and Michele's guidance. In the ring, I represent the barn and the horse and the owner. Some riders feel the pressure more than others.

I do all this because my six-year-old self used to sit on a swing and pretend I was in the saddle at a competition, and this is what I wanted more than anything else in the world. It's a phenomenally expensive sport. If you don't have a lot of money, you need intense motivation and the capacity for very hard work. It's my weakness, and my strength.

I love showing horses for two reasons. The first is sheer sensation: the adrenaline from manageable fear; hope bubbling at the possibility of success; the first step into the ring, when everything goes quiet; the floaty feeling as the horse and I travel across the ground. I'm in a different world, surrounded by bright flowers and colorful rails and soft footing. It's pretty, it's perfect, the thrill of something mattering.

The second reason is for the attention. I love to perform. I love having everyone's eyes on me. I love to show off in an acceptable manner. Picking up the canter and confidently developing a good pace says, *Look at me.* I know I look good on a horse. I have the right body, the right posture, strength, and finesse.

Of course, I make mistakes. Lots. But as Leslie always says, "It's not what happens, it's how you handle it." Let the world see a remarkable recovery, and the mistake fades from memory.

I love being judged. Because go ahead, judge me on my performance. Then the judging of my mental weaknesses, my failure at life, my character flaws, stops. And what a relief that, after completing a course, I can leave the ring and just walk away.

Winning makes me want more, and losing makes me want to try again. I can handle—even welcome—harsh criticism when it comes to my riding. It's the exact opposite of how I respond in my personal life.

Michele is the perfect trainer for me. She has the ability to slice into a person's soul, but she does so in a precisely calculated fashion. Conversely, a compliment from her can lift me up for days. Her intensity is what I love about her.

I don't consider myself the best of riders, and Michele would probably agree. But winning isn't about being the best. It's about being better than those you are competing against. Do enough showing, and eventually, you will get a blue ribbon by default.

That said, I don't ignore facts, and the fact is, I win. A lot: the Monarch International North America Adult Equitation Championships. The Nation Marshall and Sterling Medal Finals. The Connecticut Hunter/Jumper Association Finals. I could go on. I've had good horses and good training; I listen to instructions and to the horse. And perhaps I have a little skill. But really, I win because of who Michele and I are when we work together.

At my first major end-of-year competition, I was so intimidated, shaking so badly, that I could barely hold the reins. But in the show ring, I rewound to the beginning of Michele's instructions and pressed play. Hers is a strong voice—academic, offering tons of detail, and hard to ignore if you can stomach it. It was with me every step. As for the rest, I allowed the horse to take over, and allowed my muscles to replicate their training.

By the time I exited the ring, I was so happy it was over, it was almost impossible for me to register that I had made the cutoff for the prestigious second round—and that I was going to have to do the whole thing over again, this time on a different course. Michele dragged me, still reeling, back to the warm-up ring. She launched straight into more instruction.

"The jump away from the in-gate—the judges will be looking for a full-gallop approach. It will be hard; the horses won't want to pick up the pace away from home. To do it properly, you won't be able to slow down to calculate the strides to ensure a smooth takeoff distance. You'll have to ride at it aggressively and trust that it will work out as long as you don't break up the rhythm."

"I think I'd like to ride it just a little more conservatively," I suggested. "I may sacrifice the right pace, but an average jump could still get me into the ribbons, as opposed to blowing it completely."

"No. Absolutely no. Not good enough. There are two possible ways you'll come out of that ring. You'll nail the jump and win, or bomb the jump and lose. I'd rather you risk it all. I don't want just any ribbon."

It was my first time competing at this level. I'd have killed for any kind of placing. But deep down, Michele and I are born from the same fire.

Even now, thinking of the predictable ending makes me want to roll my eyes—but I did win. I doubt Michele was proud. More like less irritated by me than usual.

Sitting alone in my hotel room that night, I found it much easier to keep my demons at bay. Just a few cuts were enough to silence them, as I could allow myself to relive *not failing*. Is it possible to understand that I really was happy, even as I did my best to avoid getting blood in the grout between the bathroom tiles?

The horse world requires one to be a bit of a lunatic—which I am. It's also a very hard environment in which to manage depression.

• • • • •

Early one morning, Leslie and I are practicing with June Bug. Activity whirls around us, and June Bug is only half paying attention. She's lazy by nature, though when it counts, she usually manages to dazzle the judges. But today, I can't find my rhythm, and I'm becoming increasingly frustrated. I can only go over so many more jumps before June Bug will have had enough.

"Something's not working," I whine to Leslie. "I'm not getting the right number of strides between jumps, and all the distances keep coming up wrong."

"Yes, I can see that. You need a little more pace."

I try to go faster, but without success. "Maybe there's something wrong with her," I accuse.

"There's nothing wrong. It's not that you need to go faster, but each stride needs more energy."

I keep circling and circling, trying to create the right impulsion. The sun is at the wrong angle—there are people in my way—I am getting in the way of others.

"We don't have all day!" Leslie shouts. She never shouts at me. I lose any semblance of composure, and proceed to mess up the jumps worse than before.

"Get off. This isn't helping."

Her request isn't unreasonable. Calling it quits can be a useful training tactic, but this time, Leslie is angry. She's never angry.

Back in our rental house at the end of the day, I pace around frantically. I feel very unsafe, and the pain is bubbling under the surface of my skin. I ask Jen whether I should talk to Leslie about the schooling session.

"I wouldn't. It doesn't mean anything, it's not a big deal. She's really tired. She won't even remember it tomorrow. Don't make it worse."

Jen is good at reading a situation. I'm sure she's right, but her words don't make me feel better.

I try to cut—but on occasion, it doesn't help; and this is one of those times. I can't sit still, so I get in the car and drive aimlessly. I pass a hospital and wonder whether I might be safe inside; but upon slowing, it doesn't look like somewhere I want to be.

Eventually, I end up back at the show, and spend the night in June Bug's stall. It's the only place I think I might not go crazy.

This becomes my new survival strategy. It's not comfortable; it's bright and noisy all night, and I'm dirty and tired. Hay and shavings and stone dust are perpetually embedded in my clothes and skin. But if I never leave work, I might not disintegrate in the hours in between.

"It's not a bad idea, staying at the show with the horses," Leslie says, approving. "It gives you a tangible reminder of what you value most—though at some point, you should come back to the house and sleep in a bed."

I do, yet I can't get back on solid ground. With the various new medications I'm trying, I can't even tell what sensations are physical or mental anymore. All I know is that everything hurts.

I read somewhere that you can achieve a high through manual asphyxiation. At this point, I'll try anything to feel differently. I find a rope, but I must not be doing it right, because it doesn't work. Nothing does. In a surge of anger and frustration and desperation, I gather all my prescription bottles and flush their contents down the toilet. There is no point to any of this. If I'm going to be depressed regardless, then at least this way, I'll lose the side effects and the false hope.

I feel fairly good having made this decision. The next three days are a weak approximation of fine. On the fourth day, my alarm goes off, and I bounce off the bed without thinking, somewhat ready to face the grueling day ahead.

Two steps on the way to bathroom, I collapse onto the floor—or more accurately, the room comes crashing up toward me. I'm in a warped fun house where everything zooms in and out of perspective and there is no up or down. I scramble forward, using the wall to navigate. In the bathroom, I flip on the light just in time to coordinate throwing up in the toilet. I take some deep breaths, yank on some clothes, and limp to the car.

As soon as I get outside, humidity hits me in a hot wave, and I struggle through the thickness of the air. Liquid pours off me like syrup off a melting popsicle. At work, I try to drink some coffee, but can't make myself swallow.

One of the girls is late, and therefore she will be dismissed next week. Knowing this, she slacks off. It throws off the whole system of work, requiring me to work doubly hard and supervise her every move. By noon, my limbs hurt so much, I don't know how they are all still attached and moving. I *never* get physically ill—it's my consolation prize for being a mental wreck. But this feels like something else entirely. I am being shredded from the inside out.

I can't make myself eat or drink, but I do put in an adequate performance in the show ring, even waiting until I'm off the horse to throw up again. By the afternoon, I think I'm going to die. I tell Leslie I need a doctor, and while she doesn't seem particularly concerned—I'm always hysterical about something—she does allow me to step out of the barn to make some phone calls. At a show, this is a huge concession.

My thinking is fuzzy, but suddenly it hits me: I did this to myself. I'm in withdrawal. I've been on substantial doses of anti-depressants for ten years, and I stopped everything very suddenly four days ago. Stupid—dangerous—thoughtless.

I'm not sure what I'm supposed to do now. I need to call Jessica, but I doubt she'll want to help me after what I've done. Across the street from the barn is a small forest. I drag myself behind the trees and out of sight. Relieved to be alone, I lie down on the ground and inhale the scents of grass and pine. Maybe I should give in—rest here peacefully until I decompose.

I curl into the fetal position with my cell phone in my hand, dial Jessica's number, and hit the call button. It occurs to me that I spend a lot of my life in this position, gripping my phone like a lifeline. The circumstances and locations in which I find myself vary, but fundamentally, nothing changes.

I peer up though the tall trees, clouds and dizziness floating by. Jessica picks up.

Words scatter incoherently out of my mouth. "I have a problem. I know it's bad. You said not to make any changes to my medication without consulting you. I guess I didn't really see it as a change. I'm not usually like this; I'm good at following directions. I don't know what I was thinking. I got upset. I promise I'll do better, but now I don't know what to do and I think I might die."

"Okay, tell me what happened." She doesn't sound angry yet. Encouraged, I go on.

"Four days ago, I stopped taking all the meds. It's not because I don't trust you. It's me. I'm incorrigible. I'm always going to be depressed, so I might as well not add all these side effects. But now I'm dying."

"Well," Jessica says calmly. "You're not dying. You're going through withdrawal. It's fully reversible."

"I'm sorry!" I repeat.

"It's fine. We can work this out. These things happen." We can? They do? I need punishment, not sympathy. I allow myself a second of hope as I claw my nails into the soil.

"You're going to take a partial dose of your original antidepressant now, and then again tomorrow. We'll stick with that for now, and when you get home, we'll talk about how to move forward. You should start feeling better almost right away."

"Thank you. Thank you so much. I promise I'll be more careful in the future."

"I understand. It was a mistake, and I'm sure you won't repeat it. And I'm sorry you felt poorly enough to reach that point. Let's talk about how we're going to keep you safe for the rest of the show."

"Maybe I need to be locked up."

"You'd like me to look into a hospital?"

"Yes. No. I don't know. I have to work."

"This might be more important."

"Nothing is. I'm at a show."

We discuss how I'm going to make it through the next few days. I am endlessly grateful.

I extricate myself from the forest and, covered in debris, drag myself back to civilization. In my car I find some old medication, and within thirty minutes I'm back to what I know: plain depression. I take poison that does not help, but without which I feel worse. Contrition compels my good behavior.

Leslie is busy, so I try to gain comfort by watching her. She is a human chameleon, not exactly blending into her surroundings, but transforming into what those in her proximity need. This is what she does for me, holding my hand as I cross through the wildfire of daily existence, never diminishing my fear even when there is no fire, only the threat of smoke in the distance.

●●●●●

Finally, the last day of the last show of the season arrives. We don't have many horses competing today, so it's just me and our trainers. I'm very close to the comparatively easy workload at home. I'm worn down, but at least the end of the summer is mere hours away. Once I'm back in Connecticut, I'll try again to find a pill that might help.

It's still quite early, and I am walking a pony around the grounds to stretch its legs when Michele calls.

"We're running late. Leslie's truck was in an accident."

Leslie's *truck?* By itself? *Like it got hit while parked or something?*

"Umm, that's not good. What about Leslie?"

"She's fine," Michele answers crisply, and hangs up.

That's all I really care about. I continue my walk, and make it back to the barn before another trainer comes running over.

"We saw the accident on the way in! It was horrible! We tried to stop, but the police wouldn't let us stay. Is Leslie really okay?" she asks frantically.

My heart jumps, but I'm confused and weary. "I think so. What do you know?"

She looks upset. "I guess a driver ran her off the road. It looked like the truck flipped more than once. It was crushed—completely crushed—but someone said she was able to crawl out and was refusing to get in the ambulance. They said something about a concussion and a shoulder injury."

I nod as if I know this already, then mumble something about needing to be alone and fall into the nearest stall.

"If any of you need anything . . ." I hear her say.

I sink into the dusty shavings, dizzy, horrified, and sick. This isn't how it works. Leslie is invincible. A world where this might not be so is beyond my ability to process. I don't have the capacity for feelings this big, so they manifest as hollow shock.

I try to call Michele, and Leslie, but no one picks up. So I close my eyes and try to stop fighting the screeching in my head.

About an hour later, the pair of them come walking in. Leslie is smiling—freshly showered, nicely dressed, smelling of shampoo and light perfume. A few cuts are scattered across her face, but she looks otherwise unharmed.

For once in my life, I don't think words can hold the appropriate weight, so I do something I never do. I hug her.

I can feel her grinning as she whispers, "It's okay, baby. I'm fine. You're fine."

It's true. I am fine now—because this is how it is supposed to work. Leslie is the one who makes things better. I would do anything for her, but when it comes down to it, I don't know how.

I learn that the car hit her while she was on the way to get coffee. If Michele had been with her, they say she would not have survived.

Leslie asks whether I want to see photos of the incredible wreckage. I yelp and recoil. *No. Absolutely not.*

I'm still shaken. During the day, I forget how to do my job, and Michele patiently reminds me over and over. The drive home gives my mind too much freedom. It's not that I don't understand the fragility of life. It's not that I think bad things can only happen to people I don't know. Even at my lowest, I know it always could be worse. This is what I do learn: pain felt on behalf of what you love far exceeds what you feel on behalf of yourself. It opens up a whole new dimension of horror. I can stand my own pain, but not Leslie's.

It's not a brand-new concept. I already understand that this is the way my parents feel about me. There's a reason I share very little of my pain with them: it would be worse for them than it is for me.

It's only a new realization insofar as the crash spins everything into a new perspective; one that is far, far worse.

When I pull into my driveway, something inside me breaks. Suddenly, I am sobbing so intensely I think I might split in two. It's as if a primal force has possessed me. I can't breathe; I can't move; I can't think. The only thing I seem to be able to do is call Leslie. Even then, I can't speak.

"Why don't you come over? I'm still up!" Leslie says. She

sounds tired, but cheerful. Only Leslie could sound cheerful after crawling through raining glass out of a flipped truck.

"You'll feel better if you can see that I really am fine." I wish it wasn't always about how *I* feel, but it always is.

It's late when I drive over. Leslie is eating yogurt in her kitchen, and I stagger along the wall toward her, but I don't make it. Instead I slide to the floor and stay there, sprawled where I have fallen, and look up at her through a stream of never-ending tears. The scrapes on her face are too real.

"See?" Leslie says happily. "We're both here."

"Why am *I* the one who's falling apart?" I stammer.

"Well, I'm the lucky one—to still be alive. Really, you're lucky too, because you could have lost me but didn't. Maybe I'm meant to be here."

I feel myself sinking into a bottomless abyss. "What's wrong with me?" I breathe. "You got hurt, and all I can think is how much it hurts me."

"You know, I'm no psychologist, but I think there may be some kind of regression at work here. When confronted with something like this, you revert to the mindset of a young child who can't comprehend that her protector is not invincible. You can't make sense of it, and so that ends up generating a bunch of crazy emotions. But there's nothing wrong with you." How is it that she can even make someone like me seem manageable?

We stay in the kitchen for a long time, until I've cried so much my eyes swell shut. We laugh at how silly I look, and I try to put some of the pieces back together, thinking I might survive one more day.

• • • • •

Jessica and I keep working on finding a medication that works for me. In the distant future, her knowledge and my perseverance do prevail. However, I know that while "happy pills" can help me, they'll never truly fix me. Who I am now is the result of years of maladaptive coping skills, varying degrees of pain, and faulty attachment patterns. I fell off the right path a long time ago, and have been lost for so long, I've gouged trenches in all the wrong directions. By now, the healthy road is so overgrown that I can't find it, and all my new attempts at navigating are guided by the defective, looping thought patterns I've worn into the ground.

8. The Move

Fall sets in, and the children go back to school. My work schedule becomes a little easier. I try not to think about the upcoming winter season in Florida, but its shadow clings to me.

One day, I find myself with Leslie in her office after we've finished our work.

"You know, El, you don't have to go to Florida. I'm going to give you that choice this year. There will be enough work here to keep you busy. You've had a hard year, and at a certain point, you have to ask if it's a good time to put yourself in a stressful situation. Going to Florida might be the right thing for you, or it might not, but there's no pressure either way. I just want you to know you have options."

The words manage to penetrate the fog that permanently inhabits my brain. I love options for the comfort and control they provide. "Really?"

"Yup. Absolutely."

"But what will Jen think? Will it be okay with her?" As the barn manager, Jen needs to be included in these decisions.

"Actually, it was her idea. I was having lunch with her and Michele last week. She thought going to Florida might be too much for you to handle this year."

"Seriously? And Michele?"

"Michele's on board, too. We all want what's best for you."

"Wow. Thank you so much."

"No problem. And remember, it's up to you to decide."

I drive home in the cold and dreary darkness, the car's headlights unable to pick up any color, shades of gray the only differentiations between the road and the snow and the shifting shapes of other cars sliding through the night. I feel an unfamiliar sense of elation. The pain lifts slightly. I have forgotten what this is like; the pain is so deeply entrenched in who I have become.

It isn't about going to Florida or not. It isn't about the freedom of having a choice. It is because I have been heard. The people I work with understand me. All the times I have not been taken seriously have piled up in my mind like layers upon layers of bricks, dragging me further down. Now, in this moment, the pressure shifts. My coworkers trust me enough to know that only I can gauge how much I can withstand. I am filled with respect and gratitude for each of them. Perhaps this type of validation is all I need in order to feel better.

After a few hours, however, the excitement wears off. I still appreciate the choice, but now I don't know what to do with it. Now I actually have to decide.

Staying home undoubtedly means letting the depression win. I also can't conceive of spending an entire season without Leslie. It takes me a week to recover if she goes away for a weekend. Without her, I can see myself falling deeper and deeper into a state of stagnation. And I love to show. A great course, a top ribbon, the connection between the animal and myself—these are things worth fighting for, things that make going to Florida worthwhile.

On the other hand, I am always less safe when I'm away from home. The work in Florida is demanding: fourteen-hour days seven days a week, with little room for error and a high standard to uphold. The idea of putting down that weight is tempting.

The decision tortures me. I see it as a choice between happiness and unhappiness, but I can't figure out which option is which.

I understand now that depression doesn't give you that kind of choice. Contributing factors can make one option better or worse than another, but few offer a clear crossroad toward or away from the illness.

As infuriated as I am at myself, I begin to understand that I'm incapable of making decisions. Instead, I put it off. We don't leave for Florida until after Christmas, so I still have two more months before I have to choose.

•••••

I thought I understood depression. It's been my unwanted friend on and off for twenty years. I have no unit of measurement, no accurate test to confirm or deny our relationship. But at a fundamental level, I do know this: I know the difference between being depressed and being upset, between the emotional fluctuations of life and those caused by the illness. They may be intertwined or outwardly similar, their interplay complicated and subjective; but I am a self-appointed expert.

But despite my expertise, I am still not prepared for my first real depressive episode.

It starts slowly, with small irregularities. I am in a stall, brushing a horse, about to put on his boots for an upcoming ride, when inexplicably, I sink into the clean and crispy bed of shavings beneath me and sit there, a complete cessation of movement. After a few minutes, I tell myself to get up and keep working. I convince myself it was no big deal.

But then it starts happening all the time. The periods of immobility become longer. Still, I'm not too concerned. I figure this is simply an alternate symptom of depression, not an intensification of the illness.

But it *is* different. My depression's previous character has always been defined by pain, discomfort, restlessness. To outmaneuver it, I must remain in constant motion. I overachieve to restore balance.

This stagnation, the more typical presentation of depression, surprises me. The periods of immobility become more frequent, while actively engaging with the world becomes more difficult. I become efficient out of necessity, trying to work out the minimum amount of movement required to compete each task. I am accustomed to being the person who goes the extra mile, but now I calculate how many corners I can cut. My brain screams in outrage and horror, trying frantically to produce motivational guilt, but the screams don't carry. I can no longer function in any other way.

Working becomes so difficult that I create a system of bribery. If I can accomplish a certain number of things in a reasonable timeframe, I earn a moment or two of rest. If I am especially productive, I am allowed to lie down for a minute. I sneak to an empty stall and collapse onto the floor, allowing my body to do what it longs to do all day.

I can't say how much cumulative time I spend in the dark, lost storeroom where we keep old and broken equipment. I nest among cracked water buckets and a tarp covered in a thick layer of dirt and animal droppings, my nose infiltrated by the smell of mold and decay. I belong in this graveyard of entities that have lost all value and function, yet for unknown reasons will not be thrown away entirely.

I know it's strange; I know it's pathetic; but it becomes my new version of normal. It's okay that I collapse once every half hour. I'm like a jack-in-a-box. I live in fear of being caught and having to explain why I am nestled among the rusty shovels, but it never happens. Still, this fear is what drives me to get up. Otherwise, I might stay with my broken toys forever.

The two-minute walk from the barn to the ring, one I make fifteen times a day, becomes my nemesis. There is a small hill along the path, and each ascent becomes akin to climbing Everest, only without the adrenaline rush or sense of accomplishment when I reach the top. Each time I'm faced with it, I cannot possibly fathom managing the climb. All my previous successes become meaningless. I am the girl who spent a year doing daily hill sprints while training for a triathlon—on real hills, for hours, for *fun*. And now, this is the hill that will ruin me. I stand at its base, studying the sandy path made by the plow; the rock jutting out approximately halfway from the top; the sad, naked trees heavy with colorless snow. And I think: *Why? Why anything?*

My posture begins to change. Everything caves inward—my shoulders, my head, my stomach. I fight it. I do not want to become a stooped old lady at thirty. I force my shoulders back, willing the muscles to remember where they should be. I am an athlete; muscle memory my friend. But it doesn't work. Every time I try to straighten up, I feel tendons tearing, and immediately they pull inward, seeking the slack of a rubber band. My body curls further into itself, as if trying to disappear through an invisible center of gravity, the pain in my core sucking me in.

My whole upper body begins to tilt forward to the point that I risk toppling over. I put on more and more layers of clothing, huge jackets and sweaters to hide the transformation. I will not be able to explain myself if I am questioned. In the presence of others, I hold my breath and force myself backward just enough to avert suspicion. *It's the cold,* I say. Everyone knows I'm always cold.

But it's easier just to avoid people. Perhaps this is why depressed people isolate themselves—not to avoid the effort of interaction, but because they are embarrassed by that which cannot be explained to others.

It is impossible to cover up everything; it's simply too much work. For the most part I am able to hide my state from the clients, but not from the other employees. I walk into the tack room and burst into tears. They ask me questions, and I remain silent, unable to respond in any way. I require brief time-outs in which to regain composure. Often, I can be found propped against a wall, sobbing into the phone, with Leslie patiently listening on the other end.

This is who I am now.

Without emotion, I understand that I have become a parody, an actor playing a part poorly—but my stage is reality, and I am not acting. If I had the energy, I could write a theatrical comedy; I am that ridiculous.

There are some personal rules that I follow, even as I let so many others go. I must show up on time, and my work must be completed adequately—even though I hate the word "adequate." I will always take exceptional care of June Bug. The bunnies must be fed at the same time each morning, their litter boxes cleaned, their little worlds not affected in any way by my gradual demise. I must answer my parents' phone calls to let them know I am still alive. I know that if I ever cross any of these lines, my life is officially over. I am proud to say that I never do.

I hear that people in the severe throes of depression can't get out of bed. They stay there for days, not showering, not eating—or eating too much. I feel ashamed that my depression is not severe enough to reach that level. Perhaps then I would have something worth complaining about. But no—I get up; I shower; I eat the right amount. I function well enough that the average person has no idea there is something wrong—to the point that even I start questioning whether there really is something wrong, or whether I am simply weak.

That isn't to say that there aren't some mornings where getting up seems untenable. On these days, I find that in order to move myself to action, I need to access guilt—the guilt I will feel over failing to fulfill my responsibilities if I give in and stay in bed. As I lie there, I try over and over to summon more than the guilt's distant echo. If that fails, I use a litany of berating self-talk to generate enough energy to push myself off the mattress. Sometimes I slither onto the floor and crawl to the treadmill, which I use to drag myself into a standing position and shuffle my useless feet into action. Athletes cannot be depressed.

I decide I need to limit the number of horses I ride in a day. It's the ultimate failure. It physically hurts to remember who I was before—someone who thrived on hard work and long hours and everything related to horses. Now there is no *wanting*, only *forcing*. It's a slight reprieve, riding less, but I'm not sure it's worth the self-recrimination.

Usually, riding helps with the depression. I find comfort in the physical movements of being on a horse, as if the rocking sensation gently jolts me back to life with the animal's every step. When a rider's form is correct, her angles and balance correspond with those of her horse, offering an unparalleled unity with the animal—with life. Whenever I ride, I put myself in a position—both physically and psychologically—to get the best out of the horse by listening, contributing, restructuring, and reinforcing desired behavior. If I do my job well, the animal can take this experience, this knowledge, and apply it to any other situation it might later face.

Riding a horse involves more than movement. It's a dialogue, a conversation that requires a type of empathy I can't always generate with humans.

I know I'm far gone when the movement becomes unpleasant; when I'm no longer interested in communication.

Evenings present a challenge of a different nature.

Mornings have always been my best time, when I feel the lightest, the most energetic and motivated. During the day, I try to immerse myself fully in whatever I am doing. But nights are a different story. All my life, I've had what I've termed "the evening problem"—a feeling of impending doom and unease that ranges from mild to intense, and which is most prominent in the evenings. It's as if my depression comes to life as the sun goes down. I can feel it vibrating inside me as I move through evening chores. If I try to read, it peeks at me through the words. Somehow, I always know it's there, even in sleep.

Despite this problem, my evenings used to be tolerable, if unpleasant. Now I fall apart rapidly and intensely as the sun goes down. The decline is consistent and inevitable, a dull, dark pain starting at my core and slowly radiating outward.

Even worse, the evening problem begins to manifest earlier and earlier in the afternoon. Soon, it starts in the morning, and becomes gradually worse throughout the day. The last few hours of work become so taxing that for weeks I come home, open the door, drag both feet into the apartment, and collapse onto the floor. The heating has just come on, and my cozy home folds around me, trying its best to keep me safe. I cry so much and for so long into the wood floor of my foyer that it leaves a watermark. When I notice it forming, I start keeping a towel by the front door.

On a good night I am eventually able to crawl into bed. Sometimes this takes hours of effort, using one limb at a time, because manipulating a combination of appendages is too much. Sometimes I summon a tremendous burst of energy and make it to bed in three big leaps—a move that leaves me breathless for an hour. I compare it to ripping a Band-Aid off slowly, or all at once.

On a bad night, I simply stay on the floor.

During this time, there is no dialogue. When I must give my input on work-related matters, I text, or try to use as few words as possible. Whenever someone speaks to me, I stare at them for so long, trying to produce a response, that they sometimes ask me if they've said something odd or incomprehensible. I don't like making eye contact with people, but I find that if I look away, the resolve to speak leaves me. I slur my words like a drunk.

The chasm between me and safety is now so great, I can't even see the other side. It remains a foreign land, forever unattainable.

Despite all this, I maintain one connection to the universe, one that keeps me from retreating into permanent, irreversible stagnation: I email Leslie. Constantly. Sometimes five times an evening. To her credit, she answers almost all my emails with a short reply, which lets me know I'm not alone. The exchanges further fuel my obsession with her, and continue to blur the boundaries of normal communication; but they also keep me engaged.

the pain is killing me i want to die i can't do this anymore

Yes you can, you are stronger than you think

i used to enjoy work and love riding and now that's gone forever

Not forever

there is no point I am so useless you must hate me

Never hate

the evening will never end I am trapped in its hell and it hurts too much to sleep

It will be morning soon

Leslie and I are both big readers, and she suggests I try losing—or finding—myself in the pages of a good book. I try, but something terrible happens: I cannot read. My eyes move along the contours of the words, and I recognize some of them, but I can't put them together. I try over and over, but my brain forgets the first few words, and then the next ones don't make any sense. It's exhausting just holding the book, staring at the unending string of letters. Why would anyone want to do this? Why bother?

"I can't read anymore. It's too much work to hold all those sentences in my head."

"Try something shorter. An article," Leslie suggests.

I do. It's a fraction less difficult, especially if there are pictures, which give me a general idea of what the article is about. But there is simply no point. It's all just more effort I can't afford.

"I need you to try."

"I don't have a book. How could I pick one? Nothing is interesting. I can't even get through the synopsis."

"I'll find you one. You will read two pages a day. I don't care how long it takes or whether you process any of it, but you will look at two pages every day. I will watch you do it. I will hold you accountable."

I try again, but the book Leslie chooses falls from my hands before the two pages are up. I try placing the book on the ground, but my head falls facedown onto the paper. I'm not sure if inhaling the book counts as reading. All this effort for nothing but defeat.

"I'm going to read the first page to you. You don't even have to listen. Just exist. Then you will look at the second page for one minute."

"'Kay."

Using full words is a waste of my scarce recourses. I lie comatose as Leslie reads. I feel like Helen Keller. I don't hear words or sentences, but I hear Leslie's voice, and something deep inside me responds; the rhythm and sounds shave the sharpest edges off the pain.

Sometimes I understand a few consecutive words. It's exhausting, but I can do it for Leslie. I can do it for the fleeting moment that the anguish is dulled.

The reading becomes a daily assignment, offering a fragile structure to my evenings. I have always been good at taking the compulsory nature of assignments seriously, however tenuous or arbitrary. I begin to read the two pages unsupervised. When Leslie asks whether I've read them, I receive a sense of accomplishment from being able to say yes. With no pressure to do anything but stare at the pages, and knowing that the effort will be over in a matter of minutes, I find it easier to retain a little of the content. On the day I read three pages, we cheer as if I have passed the ultimate test.

Encouraged, I continue of my own accord, managing to read a little more each day. It's all I have, and it has to be good enough.

Eventually, I process that the book Leslie has given me is *The Goldfinch*, and to this day, it remains one of my favorite books. Perhaps its value lies not only in the story, but in the fact that it's the book Leslie used to reteach me reading, and that's an invaluable gift.

Leslie gives me more books, and we talk about them. They allow us to form a multilayered connection. Leslie prefers strong characters that defy the odds with their supernatural strengths; I prefer damaged characters more broken than myself. They serve as extensions of who we are in an alternate realm, allowing us to speak about something other than my pain, and gradually I regain one of my healthiest and most effective coping strategies. My achievement doesn't change the nature of my depression, but it does provide a type of anesthetic, as well as another open channel of communication. Both of these are invaluable to me.

Despite this relative success, living in my own home becomes intolerable. During the evenings, the pain skyrockets off the charts, until eventually, I can see no way of surviving until morning.

Leslie suggests I come over for dinner sometimes. Being in her presence is my salvation. I tell myself it is not reasonable to show up at her house every evening, and continuously try to remain in my own apartment, with little to no success. Each night, I withstand the pain as long as I can—which is not very long at all—before I inevitably reach for the phone.

"I'm dying. Really this time."

"So come over."

"No. I should be able to spend one night in my own apartment without dying."

"Possibly. But maybe not tonight."

"Can I come over?"

"Of course."

I've had a room at Leslie's house since long before any of this started happening. When my obsession with safety was in its infancy, Leslie suggested I spend the night at her place if I didn't feel safe. Back then, I was cutting myself a lot in order to feel safe—while simultaneously needing to be kept safe from myself. A circular logic, but ironclad.

I never cut in Leslie's house. That's one of my rules. And I never need to.

Come autumn, I am too weak and depressed to maintain the discipline I need to stay in my own home. My brain only understands one thing: that it hurts less being with Leslie; and nothing I do or say will override that motivation. I am a drug addict telling myself, *Just one more time,* convinced that I will be strong enough to say no the next time. I tell myself that I will not get better by giving in. I tell myself not to use people—and besides, practically speaking, going to Leslie's house makes for a very long drive. But I would walk to the end of the Earth if it meant feeling even a fraction better. I would do anything.

We develop a routine that enables me to survive. Leslie makes dinner, which is good, because at this point I doubt I would go to the effort of eating if food wasn't put in front of me. She is a great cook, and claims I am the reason she is trying out new recipes—as if my presence is of some value to her.

After dinner, I wash the dishes, as if I play an actual role in this existence. Everything is comfortable. The house is well decorated and clean, and at the same time lived-in and alive, with wooden furniture and plants everywhere—although the latter have been somewhat mangled by the cat, an independent yet friendly ball of gray fur who only has eyes for Leslie.

Once I've finished with the dishes, we watch TV. The hour and a half of watching television in the evening becomes my reason to live. Leslie sits in her chair, which is directly next to the couch where I lie, pulled tightly into a ball in an attempt to become very, very little. I sink into soft cushions and hold onto the sense of peace that envelops me. If I don't move at all—don't think—don't feel—I might, for a moment, be okay.

Usually I am repelled by human contact. Even those I respect, trust, and feel safe around have this effect on me. Leslie is the only person with whom this deflection doesn't exist. This year, I am actively drawn to her, as if by some invisible pull. It is in no way sexual—I am not capable of those feelings, healthy or otherwise. Rather, this pull, or attraction, loosely defined, is pure and clean. It's gentle and soothing, the silver lining to everything else that I feel, an emotion that can momentarily hold its own against the disease inside me. It's so real, so incredibly solid and strong.

Two feet is close enough for me to receive the full effect. I can experience it from any distance, but TV time is undiluted certainty. The greater the distance, the more anxiety I feel. To be entirely truthful, no distance is close enough. It embarrasses me to have this thought, but it comes from a place of such innocence that I tolerate it. It makes me want to do whatever the opposite of hurting myself is.

Sometimes the cat deigns to join us, leaping onto Leslie's lap and demanding to be petted. Leslie loves that cat, and he loves only her. Sometimes I discreetly watch her hands stroke him. It's a reverent experience, I think, for all of us.

I fleetingly consider what it might be like to be that cat. I can't hold the thought for long; it's too discordant. Who in their healthy mind is jealous of a cat? And it surprises me for another reason: never in thirty years have I wanted to be touched. The desire for touch is foreign, and I have no concept of what it might feel like.

This is all a little overwhelming to think about. I blame it on the haze of dysfunction.

Afterward, we go into the garage so Leslie can smoke. It's cold there, and since standing is difficult, I sink onto the cement with my back against Leslie's car. We talk—sometimes about matters of deep significance, sometimes of refreshing trivialities. It's just me and her. Leslie doesn't let her daughter see her smoke, so I am unrivaled in this space.

I come to love the garage, with its smell of smoke and its

resting place for mangled plants and the bare chill rising from the concrete. Then again, I would find beauty and peace in the fiery walls of hell if Leslie were the one to lead me there.

When it comes time for bed, I am resigned. We climb the stairs and I retreat to the safety of my room, knowing as I lie down that Leslie is only a hallway away. I can fall asleep to this thought and have a fighting chance of making it through another day.

My room is not like me. It is decorated for a young girl who likes pretty pink ruffles. It used to belong to Leslie's stepdaughter, Sarah. I don't know her, but I imagine her to be my alter ego, a perfect child who is always safe and has never known anything bad. I live vicariously in the shadow of a fictional character I have created based on the block letters that spell out S-A-R-A-H across the wall.

Sarah likes being Sarah. Her bed overlooks the driveway, so Leslie can never escape without her knowledge. This is a room that can hold pain because it does not have to. It isn't marred by what I bring to it. It can't fix me, but it can tolerate me and keep me from self-destruction, which is as much as I can conceive right now. Here, I can lie in bed and imagine myself being a different child, a different teenager, a different adult—a different entity entirely. In this room, the gap to safety closes. There is still a big crack, but here, at least, the edges sometimes touch.

• • • • •

One day, while Leslie and I are at the gym—her attempt to trap me into an activity that might generate motion—she says, "You should bring your bunnies to my house. That way you won't have to drive an extra hour each morning and evening to take care of them. Bring your clothes, too. You can live with me for a while. It can be for as long as you like, but I doubt it will be forever. Until you are ready."

As with her offer to allow me to stay home from Florida, the proposal in itself is far more meaningful than the potential outcome. A joyous warmth envelops the cool apathy that has settled into my being. Leslie cares enough to suggest this. She doesn't mind me being with her all the time. I am important to her. She is my golden ticket to safety.

As with my decision about Florida, I vacillate back and forth. Riley, the older and more sensitive of my two rabbits, does not travel well. He gets carsick, and it takes him a long time to adjust to a new environment. Am I willing to sacrifice his perceived safety for my own? Additionally, at home, my rabbits do not live in cages, as they are both litter box trained. At Leslie's, I would have to confine them.

So much of my self-worth is derived from the excellent, near fanatical care I provide for my animals. What would I lose of myself if I took even the smallest part of their happiness?

I set a date for the official move—but when the day comes, I can't do it. I can't summon the energy. I can't bring myself to disrupt my bunnies' lives. I can't accept that I have fallen so far. I need permanent care. Most of all, if I move in, I'm afraid I'll never move out.

On the move-in date, I call Leslie, crying, and detail one more thing that I cannot seem to accomplish.

"It's completely fine," she says. "This isn't pass-fail, one way or another. There are no deadlines. You need to do what works for you, one day at a time, and trust that some part of you will do what is right."

I cry more, and love her more. With Leslie, everything is always more.

And so I continue to come home twice a day to nurture the part of me that is still alive: the part of me that can still take care of Riley and Echo. After work, well after the evening problem has sunk its fangs in deep, I drive home, hunched so far over the steering wheel that I have to roll my eyes upward if I want to see the road. The pain laps over me like waves on a beach—polluted, toxic waves that increase in intensity until I shiver in panic and torment.

After I take care of the bunnies, I don't feel I have fortitude to get back in the car—but I know I will. Sometimes I need to call Leslie to talk me through the walk back to the car. I hunch over the wheel, hyperventilating, but knowing that if I can get through the next thirty minutes, there will be a reprieve. I am a drug addict, drooling in anticipation. Still, we make it work.

But there are problems with this system. It works well enough in Leslie's presence, but not in her absence. Leslie travels frequently. She doesn't tell me far in advance when she has planned a trip, knowing that she will be the recipient of my hysteria in the interim; but she doesn't spring them on me either. Every time she announces she will be leaving for a while, we go through the same process. I am convinced, with no room for anything other than indestructible certainty, that she will not return. Over the last year, my already shaky grasp of object permanence has completely abandoned me. If I cannot see or hear Leslie, she does not exist.

Her patience is endless. We have the same conversation eight times a day. Her determination to help me understand my reality gives her the fortitude to go through the same concepts over and over again. About a week before a Departure, we start going through the material.

Leslie still exists, even in her physical absence.

Her leaving does not mean our relationship will change.

Our relationship is strong enough to withstand her temporary absence.

Her support is psychological, not only grounded in context.

She will return.

Nothing will change upon her return.

I can still call, email, or text.

"I hear you; I understand; but I can't make myself believe it!" I exclaim whenever she reiterates these points. "I swear I'm trying! I don't enjoy being like this. I want to learn. How do I learn?"

"The same way everyone else does—through repeating cause and effect. I leave. I come back. If it happens enough times, you'll learn to trust it."

"It's already happened enough times. I still don't learn."

"You will. You trust me, right?"

The gap is unbridgeable. I must have a structural deficit in my brain.

Leslie is leaving for a week in the Bahamas. The days leading up to the Departure escalate in pitch and volume. I bring horses to the ring to ride, but I see Leslie teaching and burst into tears. She walks to her car to get a cigarette, and the act of her walking away sends my alarm system screeching out of control. I stare at her and see nothing but what I have already lost. I am disintegrating, losing parts of me as each minute passes. My nightly emails are wild and incoherent, accusatory and mean. She fields the blows reliably and calmly.

The day Leslie is due to leave, there is no need to self-destruct, because I am already dead inside. My life has ended before she has even left.

There's a brief reprieve after she actually leaves, as if by surviving her leaving, I have gotten through the worst part. All too soon, however, I begin slipping back into despair. By the end of her trip, I have given up hope. Her reassurances that she will see me tomorrow, that the plane has landed, that she is back inside her house, that she is standing right in front of me, are all meaningless. The ties have been severed; I am too broken to acknowledge her presence. It takes about a week to cobble together the pieces of myself, gather them into some semblance of being, and accept that the person before me is not an apparition, but the one who makes the sun rise and set.

Talk about a faulty attachment style.

I hate who I am. I hate what happens to me when Leslie doesn't answer a text. I hate that I can't accept that an unanswered call is just that, and not some ultimate statement about the future of our relationship. If she tells me she's busy, I decode it to mean that she is done with me and my neediness once and for all. I reach a low point when I leave her this voicemail while she is on one of her trips:

"Are you purposely not picking up the phone? I'm slicing the razor through me, and by the time you check your messages, I will probably have bled to death."

When she calls me back, she sounds neither angry nor scared. She sounds tired.

"We were hiking. I didn't have service."

I make her tired. The next time she goes away, she asks my parents to fly in to babysit me. I don't argue. When she is gone, safety simply doesn't exist.

At some point in the faraway future, I will realize that a lot of what I did to Leslie was abusive. It shames me to know that I did the unthinkable to someone I love. Is that the way it often happens? Is abuse always black and white? How often is the perpetrator also a victim? How easy or false is it to say that the victim deserved it by enabling the abuse? How often does the abuser not realize that what he or she is doing is wrong?

To me, it's not good enough to say that Leslie was strong enough to take it, that she accepted me despite—or perhaps because of—my flaws. Some things can't be undone, or even made up for. It makes no difference what may or may not have happened to me.

• • • • •

There are two types of people in this world: those who enjoy holidays, and those who don't.

Leslie and I don't. This year, she decides we are going to celebrate and enjoy Christmas on our own terms. It will be only the three of us: Leslie, her daughter, and myself. We will not get dressed, but instead lounge around all morning and eat huge amounts of food. Jen will feed the horses in the morning, and Leslie and I will go in the afternoon. No rules, no traditions, no pretense.

Lena and I have a complicated relationship—at least on my end. Leslie doesn't hide the fact that Lena comes first—before me, before anything in the world. I understand that any other arrangement would be wrong. Is a competition with a fixed outcome still a competition? I don't believe so.

Anyway, I can't afford to waste my resources. If anything, I have more than Lena does. I have my own parents who put me first, and I have Leslie. Lena gets Leslie because of biology. I get Leslie because she chooses so. Really, Lena should be resentful of me, but I'm not sure that's ever crossed her mind. It both helps and doesn't help that she is the kindest, most empathetic person I know. A social genius, she transforms into whatever others need her to be—not due to a lacking sense of self, but because she has such a strong one. Lena has a brilliant way of drawing me from my closed-off defenses and engaging me without me realizing she's done it. It's easy to be around her; it requires no effort, and with her I know I won't be judged for what I've become. She doesn't question all the times I've showed up at her house with my eyes swollen from crying and my wrists wrapped from cutting. Sometimes I ignore her and run upstairs to hide in my room; sometimes I collapse sullenly onto the couch, and she changes the channel to something I might enjoy. She is, after all, Leslie's daughter, and I appreciate the extent of her generosity.

I am genuinely looking forward to Christmas. Christmas Eve is filled with the warm knowledge that tomorrow will be an easy day, and I will be Safe. We eat copiously and watch a movie. Then I do the dishes, and we go to bed early. The evening problem lies atop me like a heavy blanket, settling into a low-grade pain, unmoving but manageable, familiar and—almost—comforting.

The next morning carries the magical quality of wonder characteristic only of children too young to know better. The air sparkles as the sun breaks through the dewy windowpanes, and I slowly descend the stairs, my depression still gently stirred with the fogginess of sleep. Leslie is already in the kitchen, making French toast. We don't speak as she hands me a cup of coffee already drowned in cream. I sink my head onto the kitchen table, inhaling contentment.

When Lena comes downstairs, we eat together in companionable silence, the measure of comfort for three people happy simply to coexist. After breakfast, my daily energy supply is depleted, and I collapse onto the couch. I am amused to see that at seventeen, Lena still revels in the joy of receiving a stocking—and I am equally embarrassed at my own unbridled, childish glee at finding that Leslie has made one for me too, filling it with items only she would know carry special significance to me: scissors, a scrub brush, a toothbrush, hair ties, candy. It is in this moment that the strength of her unconditional love washes over me, wholly diluting the badness. This brief reprieve is the best gift of all.

I spend the rest of the morning sprawled out on the sofa, for once making no attempt to shrink from the claws of discomfort. It's still there, but quieted by the warmth and peace of my surroundings. Leslie moves about, tidying; Lena wraps gifts for her father; and I rest my beaten soul.

In the afternoon, Leslie and I go to the barn. I hope that after my infusion of strength and happiness, I might find more motivation within, but instead I am dismayed and mortified at the continued sloppiness of my work. Leslie notices, and I heat up with guilt. She is my friend, but she's also my boss, and I owe her so, so much more. In this moment, I hate myself intensely, and I begin to think she must regret the wonderful morning she has given me. Perhaps I will not be allowed back into her home. I stare dumbly at my surroundings, finding fault in every cracked piece of wood, every dirty horse blanket, every clump of hay littering the floor.

"You want salad for dinner?"

Salad is my favorite. I can only nod and marvel. "Okay. See

you at home after you've fed the bunnies," she says amicably.

Driving back to her house, I receive a text, and pull over to look at it. It's from Michele.

Have a good Christmas. I know it's been hard. You have a great support system; you'll make it through.

Christmas has found its way back to a state of miracles and joy and love—a beacon of hope during a time of torment.

• • • • •

Nothing will ever take away the magic of that special day. But as the new year begins and I fall back into my daily routine, I am covered in a heavy veil of black. It takes incredible willpower for me to complete the easiest of tasks. Simply existing becomes the most exhausting experience I have ever gone through, as if I alone am responsible for moving time. It will not happen on its own.

Even I admit that I will not be able to get through Florida in this condition. On paper, my life looks like a slow progression of success; yet psychologically, it's all a decline. I experimented with moodiness in high school, finding solace and intrigue in the dark. But as I aged, I never moved on, insisting instead on cultivating my destructive tendencies and allowing myself deeper access to the pain I felt. Now, in my thirties, that pain is inextricably woven into the fabric of my being. There is no more choice, no more possibility of escape. Logically, it must follow that by my forties, I will be a deranged lunatic among the homeless of New York; and when I reach my fifties, my persona, my illness, my lifestyle will likely render me dead.

I see only one way to escape the inevitable trajectory of my life: I must pretend I am fine. I will go to Florida, and I will be fine. I will leap blindly across the chasm, deluding myself into believing it's not really that wide, sure that if I try hard enough, I can fly.

I know it's not good when Leslie picks me up to go to the airport and I spend most of the drive crying. I want to stop time, to change things before they add up to a reality I did not create. We talk about which credit card of hers I am authorized to use down south. It is a weak subterfuge to disguise the fact that I am being shipped off to my own execution, but I play along.

9. The Beginning of the End

I take three steps into the living room of the rental house and fall onto the floor, crying. The fruity, stinging smell of carpet cleaner rises into my nose as I claw my fingers into the freshly vacuumed pattern. I don't belong in this place that welcomes me into its comfort. Everywhere is unsafe.

Leslie is in the car with Michele, driving south toward the show. I call her, not caring what terrible things Michele will think of me, but when she answers, I can't speak.

Leslie doesn't ask questions. She tells me to get in the shower, make it hot, and then stay there until I am calm enough to go to bed. I try not to see the episode as a harbinger of things to come. I still believe I can gather myself into the person I need to be.

Then, there is the incident.

It's important to remember that past experiences often shape present reactions. Deep down, I know the episode isn't a big deal. I'm willing to accept that. What is a big deal, and what I cannot accept, is the fallout. It still hurts and maybe always will.

It's the one domino that topples all the rest. They would have fallen eventually. This is simply the way it happens to play out.

We're about midway through the trip. I'm in the grocery store, in the vestibule, trying to get a cart. It's late, and I'm tired and numb from the crushing weight of simple daily tasks. The cart is stuck. I keep pulling, trying to get it free. Out of nowhere there is a man behind me, his hands gently gripping my sides.

I freeze. He runs his hands up and down my torso and starts playing with my hair. It's not until I feel his mouth on the back of my neck that I suddenly spin free—one fluid, athletic movement—and I'm bolting out the door.

He doesn't really try to stop me. I run to the car without looking back. That's it.

This year, the members of our barn are staying in two different rental houses. I drive straight past mine to Leslie's. For once, I'm not crying—instead, I'm shaking like an earthquake. A million thoughts spiral around me: I'm not sure what that was. I'm not sure why I froze, why I let it go on for a good five or ten seconds. Does that mean I wanted it? Was I curious where it was going? Worse, did I finally see my chance to be a victim of a real crime, and capitalize on it? I read once that that those who have experienced sexual assault are more likely to be revictimized, because predators can detect vulnerability. Is that what happened to me? Or did I imagine the whole thing because I'm depressed to the point of hallucinating, and because I have to prove how desperately I need to be saved?

I barge through the garage and stumble my way onto the porch, where Leslie and Michele are having late-night drinks. Incoherently, I fumble my way through the details of the event. Michele looks at me like I've finally lost my mind—or perhaps she thinks this is simply my latest ploy for attention. I tell myself she does care, under it all.

Leslie gets up and leads me inside. I stand dumbly in the kitchen, waiting for her to take charge. She pours me a glass of water, perhaps if only to have something to do.

"Go sit on the couch," she says softly. Then comes back with blankets and pillows. "I can imagine how hard that must have been for you. You can stay here for the night. Go to bed now, and we'll talk in the morning. You're going to be fine."

I thank her—and stunned and broken as I am, I believe her.

• • • • •

The next day, I go through the motions at the show. The pain inside me is very bad, but I think that as soon as I get to talk to Leslie, I'll feel better. She's busy, and I don't catch her alone until late afternoon. By this time, I am doing a poor job of faking composure.

"What do I do—what do we do—about yesterday?" I breathe the words, each one an individual effort.

"What about it?" She looks confused and drained.

"The incident. In the grocery store." Obviously.

Leslie nods slowly. "I'm not sure there's anything to do. Use a different store."

Now I'm confused. That's not the point. "But . . . we have to *do* something."

"Like what?"

I don't know. She's supposed to know that. I stare at her blankly, afraid.

"Did you get a look at him?" she asks.

"No. He was behind me and then I ran."

"You know, sometimes people bump into each other, especially when it's dark and you're tired. It's happened to me."

"But that's not what it was like. It was more than that. He touched me." It's important she understands this. It seemed she did, last night.

"That may be. Remember, you're pretty fragile right now. Take a step back, put things into perspective, and it won't seem as bad."

I'm honestly not sure what she is saying, though I sense something frighteningly heavy sinking in me. My thoughts come slower than my feelings, and I panic as I understand that Leslie thinks this conversation is over. I grasp at the first solid thought I can identify.

"I'm not safe. I need to move into your house for the rest of the show," I say quickly. What I really need, I cannot explain.

"I don't think that will be necessary. You're perfectly safe in the house you're in with the clients."

"I'd be safer with you. I'll sleep on the couch."

"I need you to stay where you are."

"But why?" She let me live in her home so much of last year—encouraged it, even welcomed it.

"The clients will ask questions."

"So I'll tell them what's going on. Or I'll make something up."

"I think everything will run more smoothly for everyone, you included, if we keep things as is. We don't even know exactly what happened."

I have run out of responses. The shock of Leslie both metaphorically and literally locking me out is too terrifying to process. I'm accustomed to her rising or falling to my wavelength, but now we are on different planes. I have no way of navigating the world alone.

With nothing else to do, I drive back to my own rental house—but I know I can't stay there. It's not safe. Maybe I'll go to the gym. That's helped in the past.

When I get to the gym, I sit in the dark parking lot and watch the rain stream down the windows. I pull my feet onto the front seat and wrap my arms around my knees. It hurts too much to move. Like so many times before, I am left with only one choice. I call Leslie.

"Hi!" She sounds friendly and upbeat. I'm relieved, but also suspicious of how she could possibly be happy.

"I . . . I don't understand," I manage.

"Okay. Tell me what it is that you don't understand, and we'll figure it out," she says, positively reasonable.

"It's that . . . it's that I don't think you believe me."

"Ah. I do believe you. I've always believed you."

"But it doesn't feel like you do!"

"That's because we're looking at the situation differently. I believe every word you've said; I just have a different interpretation."

"See! You don't believe me! You don't understand how upset I am!"

"El," she says, with a trace of smiling warmth, "I absolutely understand how upset you are. Trust me, there's no denying that. And I understand why. I know you, I know your history, and I know why this feels like such a big deal to you. But if you step back and look at things from a different angle, it might be easier on you."

"Leslie. He touched me. It's assault."

"Baby, don't think of it that way."

"That won't change what it was!"

"It will. If someone knocks into you, you can be upset about it, but it isn't the end of the world. Mistakes happen."

"You're taking his side!" I am becoming slightly hysterical.

"It's not about sides. It's about taking intentions into account, and accepting that you don't always know what someone's intention is." I can tell her patience is wearing thin, and this scares me most of all.

"You're supposed to care about me," I say weakly.

"I do, very much. I'm trying to help you. I'm just not sure what else you want from me."

That's easy. "I want you to believe me!" Again.

She doesn't sound friendly and upbeat anymore. "El, I don't know how else to say it. I believed you then; I believe you now. But I want you to think about what you're projecting onto the situation. Who are you really angry at?"

All I can do is scream—because of the frustration in her voice, and because of everything else.

"What can I do to help you?" She sounds nice again, back to her calm and practical self.

I don't have an answer. I want safety. But for the first time, I'm not sure it's something she can provide.

"Remember, this isn't only about you. Your job is to help things run seamlessly."

"It's about the clients!" I shout defiantly. "You don't want me to make waves. You want me to pretend everything's fine for them." It makes sense now. I change tactics. "I get it. I can keep quiet. For you. I'd do anything for you."

"No, El. That's not true at all. If I thought there was anything

to be done to help you, I would do it regardless of the consequences." I think I have insulted her, because she doesn't come
across as angry, just hurt.

"I want to stay in your rental house." I know I won't be able
to handle a rejection, but I have to ask anyway. I won't be able to
survive the night away from her.

"If you feel that strongly about being unsafe there, I will let
you go back home, back up north. We can say you're sick, which
is the truth."

This is generous. It's all she can give under the circumstances.
But it won't help. My fear of failure wrestles with my desire to
escape danger.

"No. I want to be a good employee. The best. Your favorite."
The words are childish, but true.

"You are. But we can always set ourselves specific goals, if
you'd like." She is clearly glad to be on a different topic. Goal setting is something we do well together.

But I am silent, because nothing either of us can say will
change anything. With her undying optimism, Leslie tells me
tomorrow will be a better day. She doesn't understand. I hang up,
sobbing uncontrollably, and watch the raindrops bleed down the
windshield. I know I'm drowning.

Did I finally dig deep enough to uncover a fundamental truth?
It seems that no matter how you dress it up, clients and their
money win every time. Leslie doesn't do well with confrontation.
She is innately invested in keeping the peace in any situation. To
that end, even ignoring a situation entirely can be a valid response.

Maybe I'm idealistic. Maybe I don't understand her motives
because I don't own a business or have a family to support. I still
feel worthless.

• • • • •

The days weld themselves into an intolerable stretch of time. Each step I take is like a hundred miles in the desert. I pant with the effort of remaining upright. The second the last person from our barn leaves for the day, I fall onto one of the horses' trunks. The pain is intolerable. I curl into a tiny ball and remain utterly motionless, trying to relax. Perhaps if I stop fighting the pain, it will back down.

It doesn't work. The pain sloshes around me like acid. I try to tense against it, willing it out; but it simply shrieks under the pressure.

I get a text message from a coworker saying I have done some minor thing wrong during work. I want to say that's the straw that breaks the camel's back—but it's already broken, staggering toward inevitable collapse.

I ignore my phone and get up to finish working. We borrowed a friend's horse for the day, and I need to return it to its barn. During the ten-minute walk, I am distracted by the animal, who snorts happily as it drags me toward home—but as I turn and head back alone after returning the horse, I perceive strange sensations. I look down at the phone in my hand, and it doesn't seem real. It's become an illusion. I get a message from a friend, but I don't bother with it; it was sent from a universe to which I no longer belong.

I keep my disembodied legs moving in the direction of our barn. The light is hazy, and there are no edges to anything. Finally, I get back and sit down. The everyday horse show scene plays out in front of me as if I am watching TV. Everything around me seems staged, like a set dressing. I wonder if I can get back in and communicate my situation, but I am receding too quickly. I wonder if this new state of dissociation is the emotional equivalent of passing out from physical pain.

The thought floats away and disperses. All I know for sure is that the idea of returning to the tangible realm is inconceivable. So when I start slipping back in, I know what to do.

I will kill myself.

I've been suicidal for some time, but I've always found enough comfort in researching methods and techniques. Until now, it was always a fantasy—I figured it always would be. I take a deep breath and, knowing it won't hurt much longer, I find the strength to get up.

I call Leslie. "I've decided I'm going to kill myself."

"No, you're not. Come over and I'll make you dinner."

"I mean it."

"El, I'm not trying to minimize the pain. But I don't believe you really want to die."

I'm too tired to argue. No one takes me seriously. No one believes me. Words don't help. Time to take action and prove everyone wrong. I say nothing.

"Get yourself over here. I'll see you soon."

I'm not upset. I'm relieved I've found a way to be right.

I call Steve, my bunny-sitter, who is perhaps even more neurotic and responsible than I am.

"Hi! I have a question. It's sort of out of the blue, but when it's the right time, it's already too late."

"Sure. No problem."

"Well, I was just wondering—if anything were to happen to me, would you be able to take the bunnies?"

"Of course!"

"Thank you. Not that anything's going to happen." I laugh a little, self-deprecating. "I just like to be prepared, you know? I have money put aside for them."

"Absolutely. I do the same. You don't need to worry. They'd be in excellent hands."

"I know. I really appreciate it."

My hypothetical suicide research comes in handy. I already know that I would never cut to die. Cutting is a life force. Hanging or drowning myself are also out of the question. Carbon monoxide is an appealing choice, but one too complicated to implement. Bridges and trains provide options, but I'm not sure I'm ready for that level of commitment. That leaves poison.

I drive to the grocery store—not quickly, not slowly. I don't need to rush or procrastinate. The pain has dulled, and that's truly all I've ever wanted. As I get out of the car and glide across the parking lot in the early dusk, I wonder how many people around the world are making the same decision I am right now.

I only need two items: a bottle of pills, and alcohol. I start with the alcohol. I don't drink, so anything with a moderate alcohol content should suffice. I must spend thirty minutes comparing and contrasting labels. It seems crucial to make the correct selection. Other shoppers come and go, making their choices; and there I am, lingering, unable to decide. Depression makes every cognitive process difficult. Perhaps I should wait until I have more energy for this endeavor. But if there's one thing I can still do, it's beat myself up until I am forced into action. Thirty-five minutes later, I settle on sparkling strawberry wine.

Now for the pills. I want painkillers, without a doubt; but the many different brands available make choosing difficult. Tylenol, Aleve, Advil, Bayer . . . my selection has to matter, though I'm not sure how or why. I compromise on generic. Then there is the strength and number of pills to consider. Extra-strength would be more effective, so I would need fewer. A hundred seems like overkill. I settle on fifty regular-strength.

I wonder if the cashier will question my purchase of these two items—I almost hope she might. However, as I suspected, people only see what they want to see. She tells me to enjoy my evening.

I get in the car. After a few tries, I manage to open the wine bottle for a sample, and am pleased to find it enjoyable. I open the aspirin and pour some into my hand. Then I sit and think.

Until now, it's been a fantasy. A reasonable course of action given my situation. The steps I've taken since leaving the show have offered a measure of relief, but this is the real crossroads. Now is the time to decide who I really am.

If I don't follow through, I'll never be taken seriously again. I would be telling the world they were right about me all along. My pain, my depression, my battle to get through each day—it really isn't all that bad. I am dramatic, too weak to face what others take in stride. Making threats devoid of content for attention.

I can't accept any of this. It isn't true. I have been fighting against these notions my entire life. What would it say about me if I could only get this far?

On the other hand, despite everything, I don't actually want to die. Perhaps it's simply instinct. Perhaps I'm a coward. Perhaps I'm just not selfish enough to do this to my parents. I have people who care about me—whom I care about. Furthermore, throughout all the pain, I've never lost my capacity to love. Does someone still capable of loving have the right to die? To me, that right is reserved for those who have lost everything. I haven't. If I proceed, what would that say about me?

The pros and cons hold equal weight. I want to live and die in perfect measures. Thoughts spin around and around in my head. What do I want? Does it matter? Do I care? Do I want to take the pills and wake up? Do I want someone to stop me? Am I looking for peace in the only place I think I can find it? Am I making a statement? Is it worth it? Am I asking for help in the only language left to me? What is the ideal outcome? Am I really a quitter? Is my hesitation a sign of weakness, or strength?

Either way, a choice will be made. Action or inaction. The only thing I know for certain is that this is not a choice I want to make. I want to be saved; I just don't know how I can be. Every time I put down the bottle, I am faced with the impossibility of staying alive.

A police cruiser pulls in four spaces down from me. I wonder if what I am doing is illegal, whether I could be arrested for attempted murder, and whether that might be such a bad thing.

I pour out five pills and swallow them, then tell myself that taking only five is making a decision to stay alive. So I take another five. And another. I figure after fifteen it might start to matter. The next handful will consolidate my decision. I decide.

I count out ten and swallow. Twenty-five, and I can't go any further. I have taken half the bottle. I get out of the car and dump the rest of the pills and alcohol onto the strip of grass that borders the parking lot, then get back in.

Now what?

I see the policeman get out of his cruiser and stand next to it. I could still reverse this decision. I could get out of the car and tell him what I've done. Would he care? Would he drive me to an ER? Maybe he would just look at me and say, "I only save people with real problems. You are pathetic."

In the end, I call Leslie.

"I was worried when I didn't hear from you. I thought you were coming for dinner."

"I did it."

"Did what?"

"Took the pills. With alcohol. I'm probably going to die."

"El." She sighs. "Where are you?"

"Supermarket parking lot. I think I might die."

"No, you won't, I'm coming to get you."

"And then what?"

"We'll see."

Leslie is coming. I have made her come. She wants to come. I am no longer responsible for myself. She can decide for me, either let me die or make me live.

Fifteen minutes later, I see Leslie pull up next to me. I am tired and dizzy, though I suspect this is not thanks to the pills so much as the alcohol and the exhaustion of making decisions. Leslie helps me into her passenger seat, then goes back to my car and retrieves the two empty bottles and my wallet.

"You smell like alcohol."

"Yes."

Leslie turns on the car's interior light and studies the empty bottle of aspirin. "Did you take all of these?"

"No."

"How many?"

"Dunno. Half?"

She continues to study the bottle, turning it over in the shadowy light. Her beautiful hands. The gesture feels intensely intimate, as if she is holding my demons and assessing whether or not they will kill me.

I curl up on the seat, resting my head against the center console. Leslie starts the car, and I settle into its motion. Being in close proximity with her always brings a calm I can achieve in no other way. *It was worth it,* I think, *regardless of what happens to me;* and I hold onto this moment.

"You feel sick?"

"Not really. Just tired."

We pull onto the main road, and through half-closed lids, I see streetlights dancing above me in the night. I want to stay like this forever, with her, in a state of the unknown.

"Where are we going?"

"Where do you want to go?"

"Nowhere."

"Okay."

At a stoplight, I glimpse Leslie studying the bottle again. It's comforting to see her holding evidence that I am not faking, caring enough to consider the situation.

I rest. When the engine is turned off, I am surprised to see that we are at Leslie's rental house. I'm not sure what I was expecting—for her to drive to an overpass and dispose of me once and for all, to help me finish what I couldn't do on my own? For her to keep driving forever so that I would always be safe, never alone, with her until my natural death? Or was I expecting the drama one sees on TV, when a car screeches to a halt under the flashing lights outside the ER and doctors and nurses come flying out to perform heroic life-saving procedures?

"I'm not getting out of the car."

"Yes, you are."

"No. It's safe here."

"You're getting out of the car."

"I'm too weak."

"Yes, but you can still come into the house."

"I don't want anyone to see me."

"That's fine. I'll take you straight to the bathroom, and you can stay there. Do you feel sick yet?"

"Not really."

"Let's go."

She leads me through the garage into the house and down a dark hallway to the bathroom, where I slowly dissolve onto the floor.

"Stay there. I'll be back."

She returns with three bottles of water. "You have ten minutes to drink all of these. I'll be back then to check."

Leslie knows what to do. She would never hurt me. I do what she orders.

I'm surprised I don't feel worse. All I can feel is the familiar internal pain. It's stronger than everything else. I throw up, but it's only water, tinged with yellow.

Leslie comes back again.

"You really drink all that water?"

"Yes."

"Good." She flushes the yellowish liquid I've produced. I slide my head from the toilet bowl to the floor, where I pull myself into the fetal position. Leslie sits next to me and leans against the wall. This is a scene from a novel, I think: the damaged and defeated girl, the older mentor standing vigil. It's not nearly as romantic as I imagined, but I love Leslie for playing her role.

What the novels don't portray accurately is that nothing has truly changed. I've altered the circumstances and venue, but the pain is exactly the same—inescapable.

Eventually, Leslie gets up and tells me she'll be back in a while. In the interim, I throw up two more times, but again, I manage to produce only water. Where are the pills? I'm becoming weary of this game. I worry about those pills. All twenty-five are still inside me, and I have no idea how much damage they might be doing. Physically, I'm tough as nails, but I also weigh very little. Later, I learn that drinking all that water was the wrong thing to do in these circumstances.

Leslie comes back, and I tell her that exactly fifty percent of my face is numb. She says that's because I've been lying on the floor for so long. I don't believe her. I have a world of experience in lying motionless on the floor all night, and this has never happened.

Leslie says it's time to go to bed, and drags me through the quiet house to the couch, where she throws a blanket over me and tucks me in. Again, I think that it was all worth it for this moment.

"Leslie?"

"Yes?"

"If I go to sleep, how do I know if I'm gonna wake up?"

"You will."

"How can you know that?"

"I just do."

"I might be dead in the morning."

"You won't be. Do you want to take tomorrow off from work?"

"Not if I'm alive."

"In that case, I'll make sure Tami knows to get you up and take you with her when she goes to the show. We'll get your car from the store after work."

"I might die."

"No."

"Goodnight."

"'Night. See you tomorrow."

To this day, I don't know how she was so certain.

Left alone, perhaps having said goodnight to the last person to see me alive, I wonder what, if anything, I should do. If I let myself fall asleep, I might never wake up. On the other hand, I don't see many other options. It has been four hours since I took the pills, and I have a metabolism like wildfire. There is no way to get rid of them now. I leave the future up to fate.

For a long time, I can't fall asleep. Half my face feels nothing at all, so I keep poking it as if it belongs to another person. Gradually, a strange ringing starts in my ears, growing louder and louder until I can hear nothing else. I try speaking, but cannot hear my voice. Later, I learn that ringing in the ears is a common consequence of an aspirin overdose—as is liver damage.

Eventually, I fall asleep. When I wake, my first feeling is one of amusement. I am alive. Leslie was right.

I get up and stagger to the kitchen, holding onto the walls and counters to stay upright. With no time to make it to the bathroom, I throw up in the garbage can. The room spins wildly around me. I might not be dead, but I feel like death. It's a pleasant distraction from everything that hurts inside.

When my colleague, Tami, comes to take me to work, I keep my eyes on her in order to make it across the parking lot, then put every ounce of effort into not being sick in her car. Working is like moving through toxic sludge. I try to focus on getting water into a bucket, but the spin of the water and the pressure of the hose is so overwhelming that I briefly pass out. All of a sudden, I am on the floor, water spraying chaotically around me. I pull myself up the wall and keep going.

By early afternoon, I notice a physical improvement. I eat an egg, and feel better still. My performance in the show ring is adequate. Later, one of the clients is heading to the supermarket, and I ask for a ride so that I can retrieve my car. On the way, we have a lovely conversation about childhood pets. The windows are rolled down, and the sun is bright. So much of my life is surreal; I'm so often existing on multiple levels.

I get back in my rental car and back on the road. This concludes my one and only experiment with death. Nothing is different. I feel no exhilaration at being alive, no insurmountable regret over my actions; but neither do I feel particularly inclined to try again.

Was it a suicide attempt? A suicidal gesture? A practice run? I'm not sure. In the end, I decide to call it plain self-harm. A new way of using physical pain to redefine and master what I cannot control. This latest episode represents a change in the pitch of my cry for help, a way to create yet another scenario for Leslie to save me, another bid for safety. It is a new way of staying alive.

With one more option exhausted, the pain revels in its success, rising into uncharted territory. I know that if I try to kill myself now, I will succeed.

And this is how I end up at the beginning, and the end—driving to a Florida emergency room and admitting myself, becoming trapped in the claws of a faulty mental health system.

Do I think a person has to hit rock bottom before beginning

to climb back up? No. I would gladly have accepted help at any point on the way down. I don't even think there is such a thing as rock bottom. There is always deeper. This just happens to be where I landed.

10. The Therapy

I am afraid. Not because I am in danger, but because my sense of hope won't die. My insides are electric, though outwardly I am composed.

Her office is like any other: a small room with a desk and places to sit. Unassuming and clean, decorated in a simple palette of beige with touches of darker colors, it is a space that has no feelings—perhaps to make allowance for mine.

Casually dressed, she fits her room. She has tight brown curls like Leslie's, although she is taller.

We greet each other and take our seats, me slumped in defeat but also wrapped in my own tension—because as I've said, there is hope where there shouldn't be any. She curls her knees up onto the chair, the informality of her posture putting me slightly at ease. Settled is the word that comes to mind.

I get to the point. "Can you help me?"

"I don't know," she answers, "although I have helped others in the past, and will continue to try to do so." Her voice is liquid, with no edges at all. She makes honesty sound inviting and kind.

"Because I've reached the end of what I can take," I say wearily, a little desperately; and it's true. I've tried death, but it wasn't for me. I've tried life, and didn't succeed. There is nowhere else to go. "I've done therapy, hospitals, programs, medication. Nothing works. Please tell me what I should do."

She takes a second to pause so that her answer doesn't seem abrupt. "It's not that straightforward. I see it as more of an integrated process, rather than a series of instructions to follow."

This is not sounding helpful, and I brace myself for frustration and disappointment.

"Stay in therapy," she suggests, "either with me, or with someone else. I can give you some referrals."

"I don't want any of this. I want a concrete plan," I insist.

She runs her hand along the arm of the chair, and I can't help envying her calm. I'm always drawn to calm.

"Then perhaps I'm not the right therapist for you. But I'm happy to work with you, and I can tell you I have quite a bit of experience with mood disorders, behavioral problems, and treating those with a history of abuse."

I marvel at how she can quietly state this in a way that inspires confidence in me, like she is offering trust.

"For today, why don't you tell me about yourself, starting however you'd like." She sounds friendly, and it's tempting to start talking, even if I see little point.

And so I do. She listens. Through her occasional comments, I can tell I am being heard and understood, which gives me a tiny and intoxicating little spark each time. When our time is up, she asks whether I want to return. I say yes, because I have nothing else.

Then I walk out of the office, gently closing the door behind me.

I am unsure what I'm feeling, certain only that I am as defeated as when I arrived. But at least I'm trying something.

• • • • •

By the time I am released from the hospital, there is only one week left of showing in Florida before we return home. But the pain is inescapable, and I have no illusions that it will get any better in a different state. I don't want to live anymore. I'm not even suicidal—there is simply no fight left in me. Still, I have to try something, because as a human being, I'm not sustainable.

I'm going to return home and wipe the slate clean. Start again. This time, however, I'm under no illusions that I can do this on my own. Like an alcoholic, I must admit that I'm powerless and hand my life over to a greater being. I need a health care professional.

I will surrender and get a new therapist who will tell me where to go from here. Nothing is off-limits. If she suggests I quit my job and move into a halfway house, heavily medicated, so be it. My only requirement is that whoever I put in charge must be someone I trust and respect. I won't blindly follow just anyone.

I realize I may need to interview many doctors until I find one who is right for me. The prospect feels daunting, but I truly have no other choice. I start calling around. Jessica, my psychiatrist, recommends someone, so I put her at the top of my list and leave an incoherent message.

Somehow, I'm surprised and unprepared when she calls me back. How can I explain my problem in a few sentences? I mumble something about being very depressed, telling her I'm a cutter, I have recently been hospitalized, and I work with horses in Connecticut, but for some reason, I'm in Florida right now. She acts as if I'm making perfect sense. She says she has experience with self-injury and knows that many equestrians travel south to show in the winter.

It's a start. I will arrive home on Monday, and we arrange to meet Tuesday morning. The anticipation provides a small incentive to keep going.

I arrive home shell-shocked, feeling like one of the walking dead, and stagger to my first appointment. We spend the next few days talking about how I got here. I'm amazed I can still enjoy talking—can still appreciate conversing with someone who isn't yet bored or frustrated by me. It comes down to the fact that I want help, I think, and this woman needs to know who I am in order to recommend a course of action.

I don't initially plan to tell her that the scar on my face was self-inflicted, but when she inquires whether it is, I find myself saying yes. I like the way she asks: lightly, in a casual tone; but respectfully, as if the answer deserves consideration but is at the same time not important at all.

I declare that I am a cutter and always will be.

"I don't think of self-injury as something you need to give up in order to get better. What I like to ask of my patients is that they try to increase the length of time between cutting incidents, or to decrease their frequency. There are times when you are going to be able to substitute a different coping skill, and there are times when you are not. But it will open you up to the possibility of occasionally reducing the tension in other ways."

I love it. She makes it clear to me that it is a victory if I don't cut, but not a failure if I do. And she understands that occasionally, I must.

"How does three days sound? Do you think you can commit to that period of time without it?"

I readily agree, because it's my turn to compromise; and in any event, I wasn't planning on cutting in the immediate future. I'm just too tired.

I keep showing up to our sessions. I think there's a good chance this therapist is the one who will be able to come up with the life-altering program I've been seeking.

She needs to know about Leslie, of course. I tell her that my constant and frantic emails to Leslie provide a passage out of the mess in my head. I tell her how much Leslie means to me, how she is able to keep me alive, and how my dependence on her is both a solution and a problem. I tell her I want to be able to help myself, but no matter what happens, I will never, ever give Leslie up.

She acknowledges that these aren't mutually exclusive, even goes as far as suggesting that the less I need Leslie, the stronger my bond with her will become. This sounds idealistic, but not inconceivable. It seems she is able to hold the essence of my relationship with Leslie in the reverence it deserves. It makes me think that I could have a similar relationship with her one day.

We talk about Florida, because so much happened there. I give a detailed account of being hospitalized against my will, and share my opinions on the lunacy of the fact that a hospital like that is considered a good environment for someone who is suicidal.

"That kind of short-term hospitalization isn't really intended to make you better. It's intended to keep you safe, to keep you from killing or hurting yourself through a single stretch of time."

Well, that certainly clarifies things. When I checked into the hospital, I was expecting treatment and help recovering from my illness, as if I were being admitted with a case of pneumonia. I never needed anyone to physically prevent me from engaging in self-harm, as self-control was never my issue. In any case, how could anyone feel safe when stripped of everything that gives them a sense of safety in the first place? And what's the point of holding someone for only a week, when their problem is life itself?

She comprehends what it was like for me in the hospital, and understands why similar treatment would never work for me in the future. We continue taking steps in the right direction.

I talk about the incident in the grocery store and how it affected me, especially by virtue of how dismissed I felt by Leslie afterward. I talk about the importance of being believed. This conversation breaks off into an awkward tangent about my confession of two years ago, when I told Leslie about the possibility of sexual abuse. I tell the her that I know Leslie believed me then. I'm not ready to talk about that earlier part of my life; I just need to mention it as context for the significance of the grocery store incident.

"El, I do believe this qualifies as an assault, which is defined as intentional unwanted touching," she says, in a neutral but not detached fashion.

"But I trust Leslie's judgment."

"I'm not asking you not to. That's too much right now. I'm simply telling you how I see things."

I respect her, but I respect Leslie more. Therapists see perpetrators and victims everywhere. Still, I get the impression she is on my side, even if I don't know which side I'm on. How does she do that? Perhaps she possesses a type of empathy I wasn't born with.

The same thing happens when I talk about my possible suicide attempt. Leslie didn't believe I intended to die, but she was exactly who I needed her to be in the aftermath. I tell her that I still don't understand my own intent.

"I appreciate the complexity of the situation, and of what was going through your mind—the confusion, the pain, the solution. There isn't always a clear line between suicidal ideation and intent. But if I had to choose, I would call what you did a suicide attempt, because I see it as being different from your episodes of cutting. You weren't sure if twenty-five aspirin would hurt you or kill you, whereas when you cut, you are very clear in its function. And while twenty-five pills is a borderline amount, you are not a large person. Incidentally, I would have recommended you go to the ER. Even if they didn't pump your stomach, they could have given you medication to prevent liver damage."

"I wanted Leslie to save me. She was right. I didn't die."

"I'm not speaking of right and wrong."

Again, I am left with the feeling that she is taking me seriously.

• • • • •

It's time. I've run out of material to discuss, and I'm ready for the next phase. My therapist understands me, and I am willing to try whatever she thinks I should do.

"I'm goal-oriented," I tell her, and cite the many attempts I've made at self-improvement. "I always achieve the goals I set, but they never turn out to be the right ones."

"I'm not sure any type of hospital setting, short- or long-term, is right for you. Even if you were to recover in that environment, the coping skills you learned there wouldn't necessarily transfer to your life. Your animals, your work, your relationship with Leslie—you need to be able to function with these elements present."

I'm impressed and relieved—both that she sees this, and that she wants to ensure we don't destroy the good in my life along with the bad.

"I don't think an outpatient program would be intense enough to give you what you're looking for, either." Again, I fully agree. "Safety is a big concern for you, especially when it comes to getting through the night. There are places, houses that offer both short-term and long-term stays that could help you with this."

I wasn't aware of such places—but I already have what they offer. Leslie's house is the safest place on earth. But in the end, staying with her is a stopgap, not a solution.

"Then there are specific courses you could try. Dialectical behavioral therapy, cognitive behavioral therapy."

"I've done them. Multiple times. They are helpful, but not enough."

"I can see how that might be the case. For you, they'd be a supplement, but not a cure."

"So what does that leave?"

"I'm not sure. I'm happy to keep seeing you. Or I could give you another referral."

"What would be the point of continuing with therapy? I've told you as much as I consider relevant. I'm not going to waste our time talking about the weather."

"People come to therapy for a number of different reasons. Some come to discuss everyday problems, some to work through a specific issue, like loss or trauma. The common denominator is that all these people are looking to change something in their lives.

"I can help with that. I have professional training. We meet for a finite time in a specific setting. Our connection isn't the same as your other day-to-day relationships. There's no give and take. Therapy is all about you."

"How will it help me?"

"That's for you to decide."

I'm not satisfied. To me, it all seems like a game, fixed, with one outcome: failure.

Still, I keep scheduling sessions, either every day or every other day, because there is nothing else, and because Leslie encourages it. I think she's relieved that she isn't the only one responsible for me now, and I owe her some freedom.

Eventually, I come to realize something significant. For this hour, in this room, with this individual, I feel safe. The realization that I am capable of feeling safe somewhere other than with Leslie is astounding, the implications far-reaching. Like the addict I am, I crave more, and no amount of it can ever be enough. I no longer care about going to therapy to improve my future—instead I go to therapy because it's safe.

Words are my allies. I love to talk, and write, and express myself; but what I learn to love even more is *being heard*. In therapy, I get to talk—repetitively, gratuitously, irrationally. It's intoxicating, and she lets me do it. I think I might never stop, and she might never make me. Her listening is active and focused, yet relaxed. When I'm grasping for an idea, she finds and phrases it with greater accuracy. She is even better with words and concepts than I am. It's affirmative, a mirroring sensation. Is this what good therapy is like? Is it good because of her? Because of me? I don't feel any better, or different. If anything, I'm worse—because now I'm attached to my therapist just as viciously as I have been to Leslie. I've doubled the problem, and now I know where this is headed.

"I'm going to use you," I warn her. I need to be clear what kind of monster I am. "Once I'm attached to someone, I don't have any limits. I become insane, and I'll drown you in my own bottomless needs. You'll try to help, and I'll keep taking until neither of us exists anymore."

She doesn't seem concerned. "It's okay to become attached to your therapist. It's healthy, and even necessary. As for maintaining boundaries, that's not your job. It's mine. You can't come and live with me. You can't email me and call me the way you do with Leslie. I won't let it become a problem, because I'll keep the necessary distance."

When she says this, I feel both better and worse.

"Having said that, I want to let you know that I'm here for you, and I'll help you in the ways I can. My capacity to help has limits, but that doesn't mean it's not real."

My mind spins. I wonder if I can understand this concept—that it isn't always one or the other.

"It's actually a good start. Right now you need Leslie to be everything, because you limit your interactions with everyone but her. Increase the social connections in your life, and you won't wear down the ones you have."

"I don't want to need more people. I want to need fewer."

"It doesn't work that way. You're always going to need people, and one day, you're going to be the person someone else needs. It's not about decreasing your dependency, but increasing your resources."

That sounds awful. I'm a slave to my addiction. I say so.

"It might feel that way at first," she goes on, "but once you learn that you have options, the anxiety surrounding your attachments will decrease. Eventually, it will fall into the background of everyday life. Think of me as your safety net for the times Leslie isn't there. That way, you don't have to fear what might happen if she's unavailable. Eventually you could have a whole network, a whole chain of people capable of helping you, and the comfort you can take in that will help make you more independent."

That's a lot to take in. Conceptually, I understand the idea, though I can't imagine it working in practice.

Inevitably, I end up talking to her about the pain. Because it's so fundamental to who I am and what my fight entails, we come up with a numerical system to help us define it. Twenty-five is the baseline, normal. Any number lower than that means I'm happy; a number under zero means I'm manic. Seventy-five represents the upper limit of what I can handle. At numbers between seventy-five and a hundred, I lose good judgment and may do something regrettable. A number over a hundred means I'm suicidal.

The system in itself won't reduce the pain, but it offers a fast and efficient way to communicate. I can put an episode into perspective and note what makes the numbers rise and fall. It allows me to take another step toward mastery.

We also spend considerable time talking about an official diagnosis. I know a label won't make much of a difference, but in some ways, I feel that a definable problem could be easier to come to terms with than adjectives such as "dysfunctional," "weird," or "crazy."

Coming up with a diagnosis is not as complicated as one might think. Even though no medical test exists to measure my mental state, to meet the criteria for having an illness, I need to display a certain number of listed symptoms, as defined by the current version of the *Diagnostic and Statistical Manual of Mental Disorders.* I am just one or two symptoms short of qualifying for bipolar disorder, as well as borderline personality disorder. I do meet the criteria for depression, though even that is not a perfect match. I most definitely have an attachment disorder. However small or arbitrary they may be, these labels provide me with something to hold onto. The real question is what to do about them, and to what extent the processes of managing, treating, and curing these illnesses will work together.

"It is absolutely possible to recover from an attachment disorder."

"What do I have to do?" I ask eagerly.

"It's not so much about what you have to do, but more of a process that happens under the right circumstances. You can relearn healthy attachment patterns from being in the right environment."

"Like in therapy?"

"That can be the right environment. You've read the research. In the case of attachment disorders, healing starts with finding a place you feel comfortable, and gradually you'll learn that you can step away from it without it disappearing. You can always come back to it, but you will need to do so less and less."

"Why didn't I learn it right in the first place? I grew up in a safe, loving environment."

"There's no simple answer. Could be brain chemistry. Or

your needs were atypical. Often it's trauma."

The theme that keeps arising from all directions.

• • • • •

One night, I have a strange experience. I am at home, in the bathroom, about to brush my teeth before going to bed. As usual, thoughts circle at random in my head—voices and ideas and concepts I've encountered during my day.

I think of her—just a passing, drifty fragment. In my mind, she says, "It's going to be okay." A not unpleasant sensation hits me like a shock. I turn to jelly, my legs buckle, and I fall to the floor. Astounded, I pull myself back up and lean on the counter, amused to learn that "weak in the knees" is more than just an expression. But what happened? Why? I feel fine—better than fine.

When I tell her about it, she says, "It's because your needs are starting to be met, and it's that powerful."

• • • • •

We reach a type of standstill. I want to continue going to therapy, but in the absence of a current crisis, I'm not sure how to structure my sessions. I'm afraid she'll lose interest, or that I have to experience a certain level of disaster to justify remaining in therapy.

I almost wish she'd ask me about the ethereal presence that perpetually lingers a few steps behind me wherever I turn. She doesn't, so I ask her some questions instead.

"I was just wondering what kind of stuff you've seen over the years. Like, bad stuff."

"Well, I spent many years working in the foster care system.

There are plenty of horror stories there. I have a lot of experience with domestic violence, all kinds of sexual abuse, sex trafficking."

"Tell me there's nothing you haven't seen before."

"It wouldn't be true. Everyone's story is different."

"What about children?" It's crucial I know about children. I am a child. I was.

"Yes, many of the cases I've worked with involved children." I want her to say more. To say that she is omniscient.

"So do you see bad children?"

"I see children who react, generally for the sake of self-preservation. Their knowledge is limited, so sometimes their behavior only makes sense within the framework available to them. Behavior that looks dysfunctional is often a product of what they've seen—a reenactment of sorts. Kids mirror what they see, good or bad. But that doesn't make their intent good or bad."

"Do you ever find yourself hating them? Judging them?"

"No, because I have the knowledge to understand."

Something rises within me—hope, respect, awe. It helps me push on.

"But what about feelings that a kid is not supposed to have? Like stuff that's wrong and bad?" I seem only to be able to use very basic, childlike terminology. I'm not sure I'm being clear enough. "Stuff that only consenting individuals are supposed to feel, like if they are over the reproductive age." *Please don't make me be more specific.*

She doesn't. "Children can and do have those feelings. It's not wrong; it's physiology. That's not my opinion; it's science."

I'm not convinced, but she's the expert. Each step along the tightrope takes me further over the chasm.

"Because I felt that. When he touched me. I know this

makes it partially my fault. Complicit." I spit out the last word, an adult word.

"No, it doesn't," she says calmly. "It's a biological reaction. When you cut an onion, it produces tears. It doesn't mean you're sad, and there's nothing you can do to prevent it."

Part of me knows this, of course, but the truth is weighed down by shame. Listening to it is comforting, though. It lifts a layer of guilt I didn't know was part of me.

She's read the book by Bessel van der Kolk—the one I studied in North Carolina. We discuss it, and it allows me to hide behind words that are not my own. She paraphrases a particular passage I like, one that discusses how trauma victims often seek to reenact their trauma in some way, not because they are damaged and enjoy degradation, but in an attempt to regain control or achieve mastery over a particular event. She matches my language and pace. I don't remember the exact words she uses, after, but I remember their cadence and flow, how they fit together naturally and self-evidently. I remember her expression and tone, which carry with them a type of gravity nested in compassion. I remember feeling appreciation and wonder that her language and delivery is enough to create a connection of such life-sustaining force between us. When I need to, I can remember this moment and hold it in my mind as eternal proof of what's possible.

This is the conversation that makes me believe it's safe to talk. Still, even when I try, I can't manage to speak the words. The necessary phrases are too heavy, too dangerous to be let out into the atmosphere. They overpower me.

But I'm too close to back down now, and despite myself, I find a way. I can't sleep, and this time it's not due to pain, but pressure—horrible and intense. Almost against my will, I take out paper and a pencil and begin to write—about how I couldn't breathe, about how he touched me. About the fear and the pleasure and the vulnerability. About the lack of control, both over him and over myself. About how I didn't want to give him what he wanted, but I couldn't help it. The responsibility this caused me to assume. The way it trickled into everyday aspects of my life. The way I know all this without a shadow of a doubt, but have no names, no places, no context. I have no evidence that anything I'm writing is even true. All I have is a pencil that can't lie. Is this the way repressed memory works? I have no idea.

Night after night, words explode onto the page. They are my conduit. Poison leaking out of me. It's not a relief. It's a terrifying, disturbing sensation. It's not me writing. I have been overtaken by a demonic force. I keep writing and writing, lead defacing the paper. I must say the same thing a hundred different ways—and eventually I can almost use a full vocabulary, consisting of words I could never say out loud—words that, when this is all over, I will never speak or write again.

I don't eat or drink or sleep. The physical deprivation tangles with the mental exhaustion, and I become such a wreck that even the pain is stunned into quiet shock.

When I'm done, I gather the hundreds of pages of debris and bring them to my next session. I want someone to bear witness. I'm just not sure what it will cost me. What is in this writing is humiliating; it portrays me as weak and sick and degraded and disgusting. Am I really willing to risk sacrificing our relationship by showing this to her? I cannot expect anyone to view me as a human being after reading this, let alone take me seriously.

In spite of myself, I hand over some of the paper at the session and endure the agony of watching it being read. The pain turns physical, and I fear I will be consumed by the flames inside me.

I watch her hand as she holds the sheets. Even after several minutes, it is still doing so. She turns them over, places the finished ones on her lap, and keeps reading. I am broken open, but also intrigued. She is holding the worst part of me, handling it in the way I am unable to. It's contaminated, toxic; but she doesn't look afraid.

When she's finished, she looks up and says simply, "This doesn't change anything."

Through my embarrassment and defeat, I feel incredible validation. I fumble to speak.

"I know it's not like factual memories or anything, just sort of what I thought. Do you think it's possible I might be wrong, or that I made it up, like nothing really happened?"

"No." I've never felt one word contain so much: gravity, kindness, strength. "But I've never thought that. I've always believed you." And it sounds true.

I apologize to her, but abstractly, I am also apologizing to Leslie, to my parents, and to myself. In response, she says, "You have nothing to apologize for," and I tentatively reach out, toward the offered absolution.

We discuss in general terms. She is careful to let me lead, though she always makes clear that she is with me intellectually and emotionally.

Unpacking the words I've produced is a process that takes a while, and I begin to find it difficult to transition between work and therapy sessions every day. I almost wish I was in a hospital so I could take more time to process; but I am used to presenting myself in one way while feeling another.

I tell Leslie about the therapy, of course, though I avoid giving specifics. This is a valuable lesson I've learned in therapy: it's not fair to assault Leslie with my darkest ideas and intentions and feelings. She's receptive and strong as iron, but that doesn't make it right. Some things need to be said to a professional, because even the toughest, most intelligent layperson isn't equipped to hear them. To this day, I feel guilty about what I put Leslie through. She claims it was never too much for her, but I know that words can damage just as much as unwanted touching.

I tell her how relieved I am that I no longer need to use her in this capacity, though still I constantly relay the struggle of being caught between intense therapy and everyday life.

We are sitting together, talking, when she says, "Do you think maybe it's time to put this stuff down? It's been weighing on you for so long. Baggage, like a suitcase. You can put it down and walk away from it. That's a choice you have. Won't that make things so much easier at work?"

I explode. The person who has understood me better than anyone for more than a decade suddenly comes up with something so insulting—so insensitive?

"I've buried this my entire life, Leslie! I'm finally dealing with it in an appropriate setting, and you want me to stop? You think that it's that simple? Just put it down?"

"El, I'm sorry. I didn't mean to minimize it. If talking about it is helping, I support the process one hundred percent. I want what's best for you—I always have. Keep working at it. I'll try to make work as easy as I can for you."

I melt back into gratitude. I love her.

Leslie and I talk about normal things from then on, and on

occasion our conversations are about her instead of me. It's not that I'm hiding anything, or that I've shut her out—just that she walked me most of the way along a very dark road, making it possible for me to trust someone else as I continued the rest of the way.

This isn't to imply that I'm cured. The summer show season begins, and after much deliberation, I decide to join the rest of the team. The work is tough, and I'm not always strong enough to handle the stress and the heightened emotions around me. My therapist checks in with me often via phone, and I'm even allowed to send her a few emails, as long as I don't abuse the privilege. I slip up a few times, but it helps to have her in the background—someone who knows what I'm going through behind the scenes.

I have a few meltdowns, during which my therapist asks me to focus on three things: eating, drinking, and sleeping. I'm not amused. If my problems could be solved that easily, I wouldn't have any problems left. Still, I comply, and am surprised to find that it helps a little—not only physically, but through its own process. Engaging in basic self-care shifts my focus from self-harm to self-preservation.

I do cut, quite a bit. She's not angry or judgmental. She accepts that this is one of my most effective, lifelong coping skills, and that I sometimes need to cut in order to continue to function.

As is often the case at shows, tensions run high, which I still do not handle well. Once, a good friend of Leslie's spends an hour berating me, tearing apart my character, hitting where I feel it the most. She tells me I routinely hurt Leslie. I should walk away, but I just stand there, listening.

When she is finally finished, I get into my car and consider suicide. But I can't do that to Leslie again; I can't ruin another show. Also, to my surprise, I realize clearly that I don't want to die.

I call my therapist and tell her everything. She asks me what's keeping me from self-destructing. I say that amid the pain and chaos is a microscopic kernel of strength deep within me, something I have never experienced before. It's effervescent, a pinprick of light. She tells me to focus on it, nurture it, take pride in it, and know that it's possible to recreate and grow it even if it recedes. It's not enough, but it's there.

She instructs me to eat something, and even though it seems impossible, I make myself do it. She checks in later to ensure I've complied, and I feel less alone. I email Leslie about the situation, and the next morning while I'm schooling a horse, she comes up to me. She places a hand on my boot and reassures me that I do not routinely hurt her. The gesture is intimate, and although I still feel defeated, I move on.

I fight my way through the rest of the summer, but by the final two weeks, I know I'm not going to survive unless I stay home. I let everyone down. It's wrong to quit so close to the end. Even Leslie is frustrated—even angry—with me, and I cut myself fairly badly. For the first time ever, the cuts become significantly infected, and I enjoy watching them fester.

The season ends with a spectacular blow. I schedule some sessions with my therapist, only for Jen to tell me I'll have to wait until the following week, when we've unpacked and reorganized and established a fixed fall schedule. Her argument truly sounds reasonable, but I'm not sure I can wait until then.

Jen has been highly supportive of my battle, but now she tells me, "You're not going to die if you wait one more week."

I go home and detonate. If I had a physical illness, would she insist I wait to see a doctor? (Probably.) If I had diabetes, would she presume I could wait a few days before my next insulin shot? I've finally found something that helps manage the pain, and someone wants to deny me access to it. No, I won't die; but what will the wait cost me?

I whine to Leslie, but she is overwhelmed after the summer, and simply reminds me to remember all the times Jen has been supportive, and that she is only doing her job. It's true, but to this day, that comment hurts because of what it represents, and because of the lifetime I have spent not being taken seriously.

Several weeks later, once everyone has recovered from the stress of the season, Jen rearranges the entire staff's schedule to accommodate my needs. I can't pretend this doesn't save my life, and it counts for so much more than one poorly expressed comment. She remains one of my biggest allies.

Now comes the turning point, the crossing into the impossible, the shattering of my own glass ceiling: the pain is finally lessening. It's still there; it still flares; but there is undeniably less of it. I don't trust the permanence of this new state, but for now, it does exist.

Naturally, I analyze it to death. Is something that has been part of me for thirty years really changeable in such a fundamental way? Can the pain continue to decrease? How, and why is it happening now?

Perhaps it's because the pain was comprised of a lifetime of balled-up feelings and sensations and ideas that had no outlet, no way of being processed and understood on my own. I'm cutting much less, but that is neither a victory nor a defeat. It's just what happens.

I'm undeniably improving, but still immensely frustrated that I need to structure and plan my life according to the availability of my attachment figures, and that I still need to baby my unchallengeable mental states. In spite of all my newfound understanding and support, I still think like a child.

When I voice these worries, my therapist tells me, "I think of it as developmental, not as a character flaw. It won't be like this forever." It's astounding how simple things are when you remove judgment and add context.

I can live with this. It's not perfect, but it's livable. That's all I ask. We reduce our sessions by one a week, but I still have a lot to work on, and the winter season in Florida is approaching.

In the end, I decide not to go to Florida this year. It's a crushing defeat, but it's the right thing to do. I've never been away from Leslie for an entire season, but I'll go to therapy every other day. However, for one of the weeks, my therapist will be gone, and I will be completely alone. It will be the ultimate test of my fragile strength.

With depression gradually taking less of a toll on me, I uncover a layer of unresolved anxiety. Leslie's, and my therapist's, temporary absences are its primary trigger. We deal with this as we would an attachment problem, trying to shift my focus away from their departures and toward the ways I can make use of the people and the activities still available to me in their absences. The hope is that if I redirect my focus enough times, I will learn that "out of sight" does not mean "out of existence," and my panic over the departure of important people in my life will lessen. My therapist also suggests I try a mild antianxiety medication, which I take as needed. I only end up using it a handful of times. Defining the problem and knowing I have a safety net is usually enough.

The day my therapist leaves, I exit her office and wander around aimlessly. I consider suicide, but I know its call is a distant echo—a security blanket, but not a real option. My parents offer to come and stay with me, but some part of me wants to see if I can manage things alone. It's a challenge, and if there is anything I can face, it's challenges. I turn it into a game, a goal. If I survive the week without my support team, it will be a personal victory of immense proportions, a real step toward independence.

Halfway through the week, I know I'm going to make it. On the last day, I drive to work with tears streaming down my face, because for once, achieving a goal has made me happy. Stronger.

My therapist and I reach the year mark. Despite worrying over whether the gesture is appropriate, I buy her a necklace of shattered glass, because she broke the glass ceiling, did the impossible. I know my interpretation of the term "glass ceiling" is not the correct one, but I hope she can unravel my meaning. A while later, she texts me. She understands. Of course she does.

• • • • •

Because life can never be simple, Leslie tells us she is closing the business. We will move a few of our clients and their horses to a larger, fancier show barn. They will have their own, new staff; but Leslie wants to make the transition with her own team. Still, she doesn't bury me under her expectations, and gives me the space I need to make my own decision.

I have reached the biggest crossroads of my life—if I don't count the decision to stop after twenty-five aspirin.

After days of unsuccessful deliberation, I head to Leslie's house, and we sit on her deck in the cool breeze of spring.

"I'm not sure if I can handle another barn, or the stress of moving and integrating," I say. "Maybe this is a sign that it's time me for me to start over. For the first time, I think I might be able to do it."

"What else would you want to do?"

"I don't know. Something easy, mindless. Maybe move south to be closer to me parents. Bag groceries. Write. Love animals. But primarily, I want to focus on my mental health. It's important. It's everything. I had the world, working for you, and it couldn't keep me functioning. I know now that therapy has a real chance of working. I want to make it my first priority."

"You know I respect you enough to let you go, if that's what you want."

"I don't know if it is! The thought of being without you is terrifying."

"El, you don't need to be without me. I'll always be here for you. Nothing will change that—certainly not physical distance."

It's a wonderful gift she's offering, and I reverently place it high on the shelf with everything else she has given me. Still, I don't know what to do. Is moving in a different direction the natural continuation of my recovery, or a baseless act of self-sabotage?

"Please tell me what to do. I trust you more than myself."

"You know I won't do that. Maybe it's time to start believing in yourself."

Leslie spends the next two hours listening to my litany of complaints and fears and ideas, and the one thought I am left with is how lucky I am to have her.

In the end, I decide to give the new barn a few months, and take it from there.

I'm doing well, all things considered, and the pain continues to quiet, if almost imperceptibly. I decide I need a reward for trying so hard; for making it this far; for not giving up, and thereby getting to this point.

It's carefully planned out. I phone my bunny contact, and six weeks later, I make the seven-hour round trip and return home carrying a miniature brown-and-white baby girl with big blue eyes: Juno. She's friendly. Riley loves her, though Echo seems skeptical of the new addition. As with the others, she is my child; but this is different. This is the first time I've had a baby. I will nurture her into the happiest, most loving and carefree being that has ever existed. She will never know anything bad. She is all mine, all me. She is safe.

The first six weeks with Juno are bliss. She litter box trains quickly. Through gentle, frequent handling and hours spent getting to know each other, she bonds closely to me, sleeping on top of my head at night and kissing me with her warm, tiny tongue. The continuous physical contact offers both of us calm and peace. Her disposition readily lends itself to helping her become the animal I am looking to shape.

Then she develops a respiratory infection. It's mild at first, but then it becomes serious. I take her to my vet, and then to a specialist. I make it clear that her suffering is unacceptable, but he reassures me we'll only treat her until further efforts no longer seem reasonable. For weeks, I stay up all night with her. She becomes apathetic and weak.

I apologize to her a million times a day. I can't keep her safe. In the long hours of darkness, a completely different type of pain surfaces: pain felt on behalf of something else. It's excruciating, but somehow outside of me, rather than lodged in my core, and it carries with it a sense of inevitability: the knowledge that it cannot and should not go away. I wish I could take this pain and turn it back into my own, but in a way, it's easier to carry this weight on behalf of something I love. My tolerance stretches endlessly for Juno, in a way it doesn't when it's only me.

I want to put her to sleep, but I can see she's fighting. How many times did I wish someone would have ended things for me despite my efforts? Would I have felt differently if I'd known I'd find help later on? I think about the answers, but I know I need to focus on what Juno might want, and not project my own warped perspective onto her. Most creatures want to live, but I've worked around animals too long not to know that it's mostly no one's fault they die. They are fragile beings that often do not reach their full lifespans.

When Juno's condition becomes desperate, I wait for the vet to open so we can put her in an oxygen chamber at the clinic. It's going to be our last attempt to save her. Later, as I lie tear-soaked next to her in bed, she slowly wriggles her front paws onto my face and delicately licks at the corners of my eyes. I'm not being sensational; this is what rabbits do to identify their friends. It's a grooming behavior. I take it to mean that she doesn't directly associate me with her suffering. I'm her mother, and she knows I love her. I couldn't give her undiluted happiness, but at least she knows she's loved.

I go to my therapist, because I finally have a real problem, rather than one that exists solely in my head. I know she can't fix Juno, but she can help with the pain. She's done it before.

This time, though, therapy doesn't work. We talk and talk, but nothing happens. I feel the same as I did when I entered the room, and my therapist has no words to help me understand. I become angry, then furious. Why won't she do what she's always done? I know I'm not being fair to her, but that doesn't stop me from expressing my frustration.

"What you're feeling isn't a bad thing," she says. "It's part of developing a healthy attachment style. You've come to the point that you realize your attachment figure is not omnipotent. Imagine the moment when a child realizes her parents are not in control of the whole world. It's disappointing, but it's true, and it doesn't mean the relationship is worthless." I see her point.

I turn to Leslie, and she is supportive in the way a true friend is. Jen and Michele are right there behind her. My parents phone constantly, and as always, offer to visit. If nothing else, I feel stronger on account of my support system. I'm not alone.

The oxygen chamber gives Juno's medication a chance to work. The vet has never seen a bunny her size tolerate such a high dose. Over the course of the next few months, she slowly improves. The day I wake up to find her bouncing up and down on my pillow, wanting to play, is the best day of my life.

Juno has scar tissue in her nasal passages due to her illness, and she will always be at risk for another infection. To date, she has been healthy for six months. Nevertheless, she's the happiest, liveliest, funniest, most loving creature I have ever come across. She worships me; I'm her entire world. She loves being held and petted, which astounds me and makes me proud anew each day. She gives me something indescribable, irreplaceable. This time, love wins.

Then there is Riley, who likes to lie in sunbeams and take his treats under the dresser to enjoy them slowly and undisturbed. Riley's final gift to me was to take care of Juno while she was sick, providing a type of comfort I could not give. He came out from under the dresser to eat with her, which encouraged her to eat as well. He lay with her in her favorite spots, licking her for hours.

Perhaps it's unrealistic, but I like to believe he encouraged her to live.

But by now, Riley is almost eight, which is old for his breed. One day I wake up and know his time has come. I take him to the vet, who accepts my decision but tells me there are still various medications we could try that might keep him comfortable a while longer. I find myself telling her I don't want that, and Riley dies peacefully in my arms.

Back in the parking lot, I fall apart, hysterically and completely. What kind of monster am I? Am I really that selfish? Did I really just kill the animal who once meant the most to me in the world? I am horrified, terrified that this is who I am; but self-destruction is not an option. I have Juno and Echo to care for at home. This is a crisis, an emergency—the first real one I've had since being in therapy. It is time to test the system.

I call my therapist. She picks up, and remains calm during the minutes I try to slide words in between breathless sobs.

"You didn't kill him," she says. "You euthanized him, and a lifetime of working with animals gave you the experience you needed to make that call. Your emotions have to play out; you have to allow yourself to grieve. You've never been selfish when it comes to your animals, and that hasn't changed. For now, focus on Juno, on Echo, and on your horses. Take care of yourself. Don't judge what you feel. Time will pull everything into perspective. I'm here for you, and so are the others in your life." It registers. She manages to break through.

I phone Leslie, my parents, and Jen. It helps. Later, while I am at work, my therapist calls to check on me. It's an invaluable gesture, and when I say that I'm okay, it's somewhat true. The system holds.

· · · · ·

My horse, June Bug, goes to another rider, in part because I failed her when I was hospitalized in Florida. This turn of events hurts, because I love her, and because I believe that all the times I did right by her should count more than the one time I didn't. But that's the horse world, and perhaps other jobs, too.

When I ask Leslie to intervene, she says that sometimes the only way she can protect herself from life is to be nonconfrontational—to accept things the way they are. More importantly, we both know that whatever our clients want supersedes everything. The few times Leslie has let me down should count less than the endless times she didn't.

The move to the new barn goes better than expected, for everyone. Even though we bring only our best horses, Leslie decides to take along a little mare, Angel, who I'm very attached to, even though she's not nearly as expensive as the other horses. I treasure the gesture. Angel proves herself by being a worthy asset.

I love the new facility. I love that I don't have to deal with any children coming for lessons. I even like the staff. Slowly, I am noticed as a rider, and receive many opportunities to show and work with quality horses. I am well enough to seize these chances and manage to fulfill most expectations. Some days I ride from dawn until dusk, and it's still hard to accept that I am one of the few people who truly loves what they do six days a week.

I reestablish my relationship with Michele, which has always centered on riding; and she continues to help me improve. We joke around and respect each other, and it's fun. I even get to know and interact meaningfully with some of the other employees. I reconnect with my mom and dad, eventually finding the strength to visit them for a few days. And for the first time in twenty years, I get through a whole summer without cutting. Cutting always was—and always will be—something I do only as needed.

It's almost impossible to understand that the pain is gone—not reduced, not manageable, but *gone*. I still live in a universe that is largely imperfect, where pain and heartbreak and a wide range of other negative emotions are normal and healthy. I couldn't deny the pain's existence, and I can't deny its absence. It may return, and then it may leave again.

How is this possible?

The pain is gone because a therapist was skilled enough to hear the voice of the poison at my core, and because she re-taught me how to live within a solid support and attachment system. Because Leslie believed in me, taught me how to trust, and was able to keep me alive long enough to receive help. Because I always had the capacity to love; because I have loving parents who, through example, taught me the value of hard work. Because there are animals.

It's gone because I have words. I believe words can hold and express anything—that they are enough, that nothing is indescribable. They carry the weight they need to, provide a connection that, for me, will never be physical. They diffuse, structure, and envelop experiences in a way that allows those experiences to be processed. They translate, and yield understanding.

It's gone because I have a good psychiatrist, and medication works for me.

And because of all this, I am safe; and that's all I ever wanted.

What Leslie remembers most vividly from this period of my life is our sunset walk through the housing complex along the golf course. What my therapist calls the most significant are the pages upon pages I wrote in pencil over the course of many late nights. My parents remember the confusing drive from North Carolina to Florida, having no idea why I had been hospitalized in the absence of a physical injury. As for me, I'm awed by the stunning black-and-white nature of my life: I was unsafe; I was in pain; and now I'm not.

What's gray, and probably always will be, is my distant past. I will never have facts—only feelings. I will never know if I fabricated the sexual abuse to give structure and meaning to my journey. Some days, I really think I did.

Acknowledgements

I'll start from the beginning: thank you to Elena for braving—and approving—the very first draft. From there the story travelled to Gotham Writers, where David, Jayelle, Josh, and Dana gave me the confidence to proceed. Next, I am endlessly grateful for everyone at Brandylane Publishers for giving *Safe* its home. Haley is a brilliant editor—dedicated, encouraging, sensitive, and thorough. Finally, thank you to my support system: my parents, Leslie, Michele, Jen, and my therapist—you made this book possible.

About the Author

credit: ESI Photography

Elspeth Roake spent her childhood on the move, between Canada, Germany, and California, before settling on the East Coast to receive a B.S. in psychology from Vassar College. She has twenty years of experience in the horse show industry, and currently lives with her bunnies in New York State. This is her first book.

CPSIA information can be obtained
at www.ICGtesting.com
Printed in the USA
BVHW031927121120
593194BV00008B/182